# CHAUCER'S NARRATIVE VOICE

*Ebbe Klitgård*

# Chaucer's Narrative Voice
# in *The Knight's Tale*

MUSEUM TUSCULANUM PRESS
UNIVERSITY OF COPENHAGEN 1995

*Chaucer's Narrative Voice in The Knight's Tale*
© 1995 by Ebbe Klitgård & Museum Tusculanum Press
Typesetting by the author
Layout by Ole Klitgaard
Set in Bembo 11/13
Photocomposed and printed by AiO Tryk a-s, Odense, Denmark
ISBN 87 7289 341 9


Published with the support of
Statens Humanistiske Forskningsråd
*(The Research Council for the Humanities)*

Museum Tusculanum Press
University of Copenhagen
Njalsgade 92
DK-2300 Copenhagen S
Denmark

# Acknowledgements

When I first started working with *The Knight's Tale* at York many years ago I had the great privilege to be supervised by Professor Derek Pearsall, now Harvard University. For that reason it has been especially rewarding for me that Professor Pearsall has read the present manuscript. I have received further comments and suggestions from Professor A. C. Spearing, University of Virginia, and I thank both heartily. These two outstanding medievalists are acknowledged throughout the book, as I quote and discuss their work. I thank also my former collaborator Lene N. Christensen and former colleagues at the University of Copenhagen for inspiring ideas. My special thanks go to Associate Professor Dorrit Einersen, Copenhagen, and Professor Graham Caie, now Glasgow University, for their ever encouraging attitude and many enlightening and enlightened comments to my work.

A number of foundations have enabled me to write this book. I thank the Danish Research Academy, The Erasmus Foundation, The Knud Højgaard Foundation, The Giese Foundation and The Sophus Berendsen Foundation for funding a six months' research visit at the University of Glasgow, and the Danish Research Council for the Humanities for their generous support in connection with publication. I also thank my publishers, *Museum Tusculanum*, and particularly Marianne Alenius for her great help and professional advice.

Finally I owe my deepest gratitude to my wife Ida, who not only is my best commentator, proofreader and adviser, but without whose inspiration and example this book would never have been written.

For Ida

# Contents

# Introduction

The most consistent complaint in reviews of modern Chaucer criticism is probably that the critic has been turning round stones that have been turned many times before. This is hardly surprising in an age where some 200 titles appear in the field every year in the U. S. and Britain alone. Even though the present century, and especially the last thirty years, have seen a great many new approaches in literary criticism, it is quite unavoidable that studies of Chaucer are so rarely unique. However, it is every critic's right to try to persuade readers that his or her study is exceptional in certain respects. Such is also my intention in this introduction.

To my knowledge there has not been a specialized study of narrative voice in *The Knight's Tale* before. In fact the critical assessment of Chaucer's narration has recently taken quite new directions, with implications for all of *The Canterbury Tales*, but none of the contributors (discussed in chapter two) have studied *The Knight's Tale* on the basis of modern narrative theory combined with comparative analysis and close reading. Many, however, have suggested guidelines for studying Chaucer in this way, and one of the first modern critics to delimit field and method was Dieter Mehl:

> Die frage nach dem Erzähler bei Chaucer stellt sich somit in erster Linie als ein stilistisch-rhetorisches, nicht als ein psychologisches oder erkenntnistheoretisches Problem dar, und sie kann im Grunde nicht ohne eine Betrachtung von Chaucers Erzählstil im ganzen behandelt werden.[1]

> Thus the question of Chaucer's narrator is first and foremost stylistic-rhetorical rather than psychological or epistemological, and it cannot really be treated without contemplating Chaucer's narrative style generally. *(My translation)*

Style and rhetoric are indeed key words in a study of my type, and the comparison with Chaucer's narration in other works is a cornerstone in this study. The general conclusion I hope to reach is one that illustrates Chaucer's narration generally through the consideration of one specific text related to other texts in the corpus.

Comparative analysis with medieval texts outside Chaucer and his direct sources has been largely avoided, but the reader's familiarity with such background as provided in J. A. Burrow's *Medieval Writers and Their Work* is assumed. The idea has been to establish the uniqueness of Chaucer's narrative voice by concentrating as much as possible on our best sources for that, his own texts. To give an illustration of my approach, I would suggest that medieval handbooks on, say, rhetoric or courtly love, or indeed contemporary literature in the genres that Chaucer writes in, mean relatively little to his poetry. We need to be familiar with these other texts to assess Chaucer's superior technique, but in his time Chaucer is always the exception. He does not follow literary recipes and never, excepting a few short poems from his youth, writes a purely conventional piece of genre poetry. I have thus chosen to refer to late medieval literary traditions and conventions only in general terms, with the exception of a brief comparison with narrative voice in popular romances (see chapter 4). The work of such scholars as Alistair Minnis on medieval conceptions of rhetoric and literature has made my choice an easier one, since this side of the literary tradition is now covered so well.

In the biennial Chaucer lecture of the New Chaucer Society, 1994, Paul Strohm remarked that no study of history can be carried out without theory, and more importantly that no theory can be applied without a sense of history.[2] The implication, obvious as it may seem, is an important one to keep in mind in Chaucer criticism, as the field has often suffered from neglect of both theory and history. Let me make it clear before going through methodological considerations in more detail that I approach my study from a basically structuralist angle with a certain 'magpie' tendency of incorporating other angles, and that my work, despite its chiefly literary focus, has affinities with the versions of historicism represented by such critics as Pearsall, Aers and Strohm.[3]

Closer specification of field and method will be undertaken in the course of the first three chapters (part I), but a final initial reservation concerns the main textual corpus of my study. *The Knight's Tale* and all other works by Chaucer are in this book synonymous with the texts printed in *The Riverside Chaucer* (gen. ed. Larry D. Benson, Boston: Houghton Mifflin, 1987). For the sake of convenience I have accepted this standard text and also avoided speculation at any great length about Chaucer's first version of the poem, the lost 'Palamon and Arcite'.

Hopefully the merits of this work are to be found in its detailed analysis and discussion, and so I do not hesitate to give a brief chapter-by-chapter guide to end the introduction. Chapter 1 explores the main directions of Chaucer criticism in the present century with an emphasis on the 'dramatic' theory of Chaucer's narration. The relationship between author, text and audience is discussed in the light of more recent theory and through examples from Chaucer's major works. In chapter 2 we turn to narration in *The Knight's Tale* more specifically. Present day critical opinions about teller and tale are reviewed, and the very foundation for operating with a Knight-persona as narrator is seriously questioned. Having established the general principles for the Chaucerian narrative voice, the methodological considerations of Chaucer's technique continue in chapter 3. Compositional features are under special scrutiny in connection with the discussion of poetic design and narrative strategy, and a model for analysis of the tale's narration is drawn up to end part I. Before the analysis based on this model (chapters 5–7) there is a chapter on narratorial self-consciousness, which takes the discussion of the narrator's presence in the tale beyond the question of general narrative stance. We see how the narrator's efforts sometimes work contrary to his ostensible intentions. Such a deliberate strategy from Chaucer is also at work in instances of humour, realism and distance, analysed in chapter 5. It is argued that these devices contrast with seriousness, high style and involvement, especially in the representations of the pagan universe (chapter 6) and the philosophical passages (chapter 7). Throughout the analysis the narrative voice is treated as the key to a general interpretation. After a summary of evidence this interpretation is put forward in the conclusion, and further perspectives on Chaucer's narrative voice are outlined.

## Notes to introduction

1. Dieter Mehl, 'Erscheinungsformen des Erzählers in Chaucers *Canterbury Tales*' in Arno Esch, ed., *Chaucer und seine Zeit. Symposium für Walter Schirmer* (Tübingen: Niemeyer, 1968). Repr. in Willi Erzgräber, ed., *Geoffrey Chaucer* (Darmstadt: Wissenschaftliche Buchgesellschaft, 1983). The quotation is from the latter edition, p 266.
2. Paul Strohm, 'Biennial Chaucer Lecture', *Ninth International Congress of the New Chaucer Society*, Dublin, 1994.
3. For the expression 'magpie tendency' see Priscilla Martin, 'Chaucer and Feminism: A Magpie View' in Juliette Dor, ed., *A Wyf Ther Was: Essays in Honour of Paule Mertens-Fonck*. Liege: University of Liege, 1992.

# Part I

# CHAPTER 1

# Chaucer's Narrative Voice: Critical Approach

[Chaucer's *Knight's Tale* possesses] language that is in the highest sense of the word poetical ... of the imagination ... of the ennobling or intense passions.[1]

> Chaucer is himself the great poetical observer of men, who in every age is born to record and eternize its acts. This he does as a master, as a father, and superior, who looks down on their little follies from the Emperor to the Miller; sometimes with severity, oftener with joke and sport.[2]

Wordsworth's statement from 1805 and Blake's description from 1809 well express sentiments that many readers of *The Canterbury Tales* today will agree in. I have chosen these two quotations as a starting point for my study, because they together express my central field of investigation, the 'poetical language' of *The Knight's Tale* and Chaucer as a 'poetical observer', both in as praiseworthy and elegant terms as I can only hope to imitate through this *academic* reassessment of Chaucer's *Knight's Tale* and its narrative voice.

I shall not attempt to survey in full the critical history of Chaucer's work, which goes back in a continuing line to his own time.[3] This would easily be another full book. However, it will be a necessary background for my discussion to outline the major critical approaches of the present century . My bias in doing so will be on perspectives directly related to my particular point of view, but a general review of the various schools and tendencies will serve as a first step towards establishing a theoretical and methodological framework. Let me stress that my outline is brief and highly selective, since its sole purpose is to serve as a frame of reference for the ensuing analysis of Chaucer's narrative voice in *The Knight's Tale*.[4]

The first shift of paradigm in Chaucer criticism this century was the work of G. L. Kittredge and especially his many times reprinted article 'Chaucer's Discussion of Marriage' from 1912. Whereas dramatic readings had been seen before (William Blake in fact gave a very lively representation of the Canterbury pilgrims in his *Descriptive Catalogue*, to give but one example), Kittredge was the first to advocate a unity of the *Tales* based on thematic, structural and dramatic links:

> Yet Chaucer's plan is clear enough. Structurally regarded, the *Canterbury Tales* is a kind of Human Comedy. From this point of view, the Pilgrims are the *dramatis personae*, and their stories are only speeches that are somewhat longer than common, ...[5]

This so-called dramatic theory has remained enormously influential and still to a large extent dominates the way *The Canterbury Tales* are read and taught, despite some obvious problems connected with any unified view of such a fragmented text. Kittredge himself in fact does not go quite as far as some of his later followers, basing his analysis on themes and character-links (I deliberately exclude structures) demonstrably present in the *Tales*, but perhaps it is a typical feature in criticism that a theory leads to over-interpretation from less able critics following suit. Certainly this is true of the major critical tendencies in the field of Chaucer.[6]

From the angle of this study the next significant step is the introduction of New Critical and later structuralist methods into Chaucer criticism, somewhat delayed in relation to other fields of literature. The two most influential critics appearing in the 1950s are E. Talbot Donaldson and Charles Muscatine. Donaldson's article 'Chaucer the pilgrim' from 1954 invents the *persona*, who is Chaucer's fictional counterpart in the *Tales*, compared by Donaldson to such characters as Swift's Gulliver, prone to being unreliable and the agent of authorial ironies. In turn the other pilgrims become *personae* in relation to their tales, a strong connection emerging between portraits in the *General Prologue* and the teller/tale relationships.[7] It will appear that Donaldson's reading is not opposed to the dramatic theory; in fact it adds just another facet to it. Donaldson set the agenda for an endless number of ironical interpretations of the *Tales*, including the long held almost unanimous agreement among critics that only three pilgrims, representative of the three estates, namely The Knight, the Parson and the Plowman, are exempt from any ironical criticisms.

Charles Muscatine's innovation in the 1950s was to combine a literary historical approach, mainly through an assessment of Chaucer's heritage from the French courtly tradition, with New Critical close reading. His view of *The Knight's Tale* as 'a poetic pageant ... expressing the nature of the noble life' must be the most quoted since its appearance in 1950. 'Form, Texture and Meaning in Chaucer's *Knight's Tale*' is in a way the first *must* to consider in any study of that tale since it is the first attempt in criticism to come to terms with the problematic poetic varieties in it. As Muscatine starts by pointing out, *The Knight's Tale* had hitherto been regarded by critics as a somewhat unsatisfactory romance.[8]

In *Chaucer and the French Tradition* from 1957 Muscatine presents what still remains, along with its other merits, one of the finest expositions of Chaucer's narrative skills. Not in direct opposition to Donaldson, Muscatine does however point to some needed modifications in Kittredge's dramatic theory:

> The relationship between tellers and tales varies, as everyone knows, from a mechanical inconsequentality to the full naturalism of the dramatic monologues. It is obvious, after allowing for the incompleteness of the plan and the evident carelessness with which some tales were assigned, that Chaucer did not seek in the tales any reportorial fidelity to the idiom of his pilgrims ... Where Chaucer mediated carefully between teller and tale, he sought not an idiomatic but a tonal and attitudinal relationship.[9]

'As everyone knows' and 'it is obvious' are expressions of a certainty that Muscatine ought perhaps to have left out, bearing in mind some types of readings that appeared then and still appear in the 'dramatic' tradition. However, he is formulating a basic stand about Chaucer's narration which is now taken for granted by the majority of critics, and which I will take issue with in more detail in chapter 2.

D. W. Robertson Jr. offers another angle on Chaucer's narrative perspective with *A Preface to Chaucer* from 1962, the major single work from the front figure in the allegorical school of Chaucer criticism. Robertson had in fact developed his ideas in articles throughout the fifties, and a work like Ralph Baldwin's *The Unity of the Canterbury Tales* from 1955 in many ways also precedes Robertson's *Preface*. Baldwin operates with Donaldson's pilgrim – poet distinction, but the 'unity' according to him is the pilgrimage as a spiritual journey, and this becomes 'the central point of the narrative, the altar stone, if you will.'[10] Robertson follows suit and establishes a full system of fixed *personae* for the pilgrim-tellers which allows them all to be filtered through an exegetic pattern of interpretation. In this way they assume the parts of characters in a Christian drama, but the rigorousness of allegorical exegesis allows for none of the colourful and richly nuanced characterization that Kittredge found represented in the pilgrims, and it is in direct opposition to the New Critics and structuralists in its bleak and serene vision of Chaucer's universe. A typical instance of the reductionism of Robertson's reading can be seen in the way he immediately dismisses Chaucer's carefully rounded character portraits as mere types:

> There are a number of exegetes in Chaucer's *Canterbury Tales*, some casually so and some professionally. Among the more prominent are the wife of Bath, the friar in the Summoner's Tale, the pardoner, and the parson. Of these, the first is hopelessly carnal and literal, the second is an arrant hypocrite, the third is aware of the spirit but defies it, and the last is, from a fourteenth-century point of view, altogether admirable.[11]

There is no denying that Robertson's study of medieval iconography in *A Preface to Chaucer* is both impressive and illuminating, but in a study concerned with narrative technique there is no further space for taking Robertson's persona-types and allegorical pastiches into consideration.

The opposed readings of the small school of allegorical critics and the bigger and more diffusely defined school of New Critics and structuralists dominated Chaucer criticism completely until the end of the 1970s, alongside traditional philology. A discussion of some of these and also more recent critical perspectives on Chaucer's narration, especially in *The Knight's Tale*, will appear in the next chapter, whereas the rest of this chapter will be an assessment of the impact of critical tendencies emerging in literary criticism and theory from the late 1960s onwards. The focus in this part will again be on narrative technique and theories of narration.

Marxist, Freudian and feminist approaches, three of the critical modes associated especially with the 1970s, had their impact on Chaucer criticism from the late 1970s onwards, often in a combination of socio-psychological analysis with a focus on women, such as the pioneer work of David Aers, *Chaucer, Langland, and the Creative Imagination* or his article with a telling title which preceded it, 'Criseyde: Woman in Medieval Society.'[12] Aers' work shows how it is possible to remain faithful to medieval contexts while still providing new and challenging angles on Chaucer, but many have been less successful, especially the Freud-inspired studies focusing on character psychology in what amounts to extremely dramatic readings with an entirely modern concept of characterization.

The New Historicist movement that grew out of the Marxist approach is now the most serious challenge to traditional approaches in Chaucer criticism, although first adopted for Renaissance studies. A detailed discussion of some New Historicist critics follows in the next chapter, but so far let me suggest that as far as narrative technique is concerned the movement has brought little new insight. This is hardly surprising, since New Historicism in a reaction against the tradition of New Criticism tends to focus largely on text-external and contextual features. Textinternal approaches, including narrative technique, are often simply sacrificed or even worse adapted straight from deconstructivist or postmodernist text theories.

The dangers inherent in uncritical applications of modern text theories to Chaucer and 14th century literature in general have been a main concern of many medievalists in the 1980s and 90s. Alistair Minnis has provided the main framework of comparison with late medieval attitudes towards the text with his *Medieval Theory of Authorship: Scholastic Literary Attitudes in the Later Middle Ages*. In a paper on 'Chaucer and Comtemporary Literary Theory' Minnis sums up his main points about medieval concepts of the role of the author, based on Aquinas' modifications of Aristotle. This leads to the following interpretative model, which I have briefly abbreviated on the basis of Minnis' formulation:

1. *Causa efficiens*
The efficient cause was the author, the person who brought the literary work from potentiality into being.

2. *Causa materialis*
The material cause was the substratum of the work, that is, the literary materials that were the writer's sources.

3. *Causa formalis*
The formal cause of the literary work was the pattern imposed by the *auctor* on his materials. ... [a] the *forma tractandi*, ... or didactic procedure; and [b] the *forma tractatus*, ... the way in which the *auctor* had structured it.

### 4. *Causa finalis*

The final cause of the work was the ultimate justification for the existence of a work, the *finis* ... the particular good that (in the opinion of the commentator) he had intended to bring about.[13]

From this model we can conclude that the *auctor* assumes a very active role in medieval literature in forming and controlling his material as craftily and purposefully as possible, and moreover that the audience response to the literary work would assume such a directed process of transmission. Alcuin Blamires quotes instances of scribes adding 'Auctor' in the margin of two manuscripts of *The Canterbury Tales*.[14] The author is thus conceived as *responsible* for the direction of his work, or at least for compiling his material, passing it on, and shaping it.

Chaucer, who was characteristically lauded by his contemporaries and early commentators for his *craftmanship* (compare Chaucer's own reference to 'moral Gower' and 'philosophical Strode', *Troilus and Criseyde*, book V, 1856–7), was acutely aware of this responsibility, as indicated by his many disclaimers and apologies when feeling urged to represent stories faithfully. A famous example is the narratorial self-consciousness displayed at the end of *The Miller's Prologue*:

> And therefore every gentil wight I preye,
> For Goddes love, demeth nat that I seye
> Of yvel entente, but for I moot reherce
> Hir tales alle, be they bettre or werse,
> Or elles falsen som of my mateere.
> And therefore, whoso list it nat yheere,
> Turne over the leef and chese another tale;
> For he shal fynde ynowe, grete and smale,
> Of storial thyng, that toucheth gentilesse,
> And eek moralitee and hoolynesse.
> Blameth nat me if that ye chese amys.
> The Millere is a cherl; ye knowe wel this.
> So was the Reve eek and othere mo,
> And harlotrie they tolden bothe two.
> Avyseth yow, and put me out of blame;
> And eek men shal nat maken ernest of game.
> (I, 3171–86)

If we compare with Minnis' model, Chaucer, or technically speaking his narrator, is in fact explicitly referring to all four *causae*: *causa efficiens* in the references to himself and his work of creation, *causa materialis* in the references to the stories he is going to render, *causa formalis* in the references to the form of the stories, the multiplicity of genres ('storial thyng, that toucheth gentilesse,' 'harlotrie,' etc.), and *causa finalis* in the reference to his 'nat ... yvel entente'. The commitment to these causes is stressed by a narratorial claim of necessarily having to be faithful to storial obligations ('for I moot reherce... or elles falsen som of my mateere'), and playfully (and conventionally) this concern is pronounced to be more important than any personal considerations, ('Blameth nat me'), while the audience is induced to share the responsibility ('if that ye chese amys'). By disclaiming responsibility for the nature of his material, Chaucer may in fact be said to suggest the implicitly assumed existence of a poetic contract.[15]

Whereas Chaucer's voice is playful here, it can also be painfully serious in expressing the authorial responsibility, as in the narratorial comments in *Troilus and Criseyde*:

For how Criseyde Troilus forsook –
Or at the leeste, how that she was unkynde –
Moot hennesforth ben matere of my book
(book IV, 15–17)

I fynde ek in stories elleswhere,
Whan through the body hurt was Diomede
Of Troilus, tho wep she many a teere
Whan that she saugh his wyde wowndes blede,
And that she tok, to kepen hym, good hede;
And for to helen hym of his sorwes smerte
Men seyn – I not – that she yaf him hire herte.
(book V, 1044–50)

Chaucer's narrative voice is at the point of despair in these examples as part of the overall strategy to evoke pathos and to excuse Criseyde, but the loyalty and responsibility towards the story goes first, even though the narrator is deliberately vague about the painful realities of his source material.

A final example will illustrate how Chaucer in all his three major works indicates authorial presence, responsibility, and awareness of a poetic contract.[16] In *The Legend of Good Women* the author's role and intention are spelled out:

> But wherefore that I spak, to yeve credence
> To bokes olde and don hem reverence,
> Is for men shulde autoritees beleve
> There as there lyth non other assay to preve
> For myn entent is, or I fro yow fare,
> The naked text in English to declare
> Of many a story, or elles many a geste,
> as autours seyn; leveth hem if you leste.
> (G, 81–88)

Here the authorial figure appears as more of a compilator or translator than a creator (in medieval terms of course two sides of the same coin), with the relatively modest intention of declaring the plain text of his sources in English. Although this may be spoken with tongue-in-cheek, most of the *Legend of Good Women* are in fact relatively close adaptions of the originals, and this is indicative of their inferiority in relation to *Troilus and Criseyde* and *The Canterbury Tales*. However, we may now recognize a pattern of poetic limitation: It appears that a medieval author may, like a modern author, take poetic licence to assume a voice different from his 'true self' (the inverted commas are unavoidable), but he cannot, unlike the modern author, escape his obligation for the direction and ultimate goal of his work. There are other clear signs in Chaucer's work that he was more than usually worried about especially one of the *causae*, the *causa finalis*. At least this will readily explain both the so-called *Palinode* of *Troilus and Criseyde* and the *Retraction* of *The Canterbury Tales,* which have so often worried critics.

Another basic difference from the modern literary situation is the literary culture of Chaucer's day, characterized by a co-existing bookish culture of manuscripts, which were read or recited, and an oral literature, performed in a number of ways, for instance song, dance, recital. Chaucer clearly belonged to the former, but the techniques of the oral tradition are part of his poetic competence, a point I shall elaborate in chapter 4. Derek Pearsall has argued convincingly that Chaucer in his career turned from being a poet-performer and 'poet of the court', as exemplified by the love poems and notably *Troilus and Criseyde*, to explicitly addressing himself to the private reader in the Canterbury Tales (cf the quotation from *The Miller's Prologue* above). According to Pearsall's estimate (and as agreed by most critics) *The Knight's Tale* belongs to a period of composition in which Chaucer was moving from one to the other, and so it is as likely to have been intended for performance as much as for solitary reading.[17]

Any valid modern theory of medieval narrative technique and of Chaucer in particular will have to consider both the general medieval theory of authorship and Chaucer's particular literary context. With a strong emphasis on the *auctor* both as creator/translator and as potentially a poet-performer, ie a direct transmitter of his own text, we may draw a picture of Chaucer as a strong authorial presence in his work. This is hardly reconcilable with the deconstructionist tendency to let the author disappear from his work, declaring that there is nothing there but the text (cf also Pearsall, pp 3–4). Moreover, that particular claim is highly problematic because there is rarely only one text in medieval literature, but rather a number of always partly unreliable manuscript versions. Witness Chaucer's awareness of this somewhat frustrating fact in his short poem 'Adam Scriveyn'. Furthermore, as Winthrop Wetherbee points out in a critique of deconstructivist criticism, the medieval text is rarely unique in another sense: a number of sources and analogues will usually have to be considered before we can assess the 'originality' of any one text.[18] As we know, copyright is a very modern phenomenon, as is fidelity to the original version in translations.

Deconstructivist and postmodernist theory has in fact been applied to Chaucer, for example by the New Historicist critic Peggy Knapp, who in 1987 duelled with Traugott Lawler in a *pro* and *con* debate on its applicability to *The Canterbury Tales*.[19] Knapp is sensibly not entirely *pro* and demonstrates awareness of the problems surrounding authorial intention. However, she also shows how Derrida in *Grammatology* tried to do away with this intentionality by focusing on how readers will respond differently to authorial intention, thus nullifying the validity and closedness of the textual illocution. In linguistic terminology this would amount to the well known intentionality of the illocutionary act as opposed to the unpredictability in principle of the perlocutionary effect. However, I would argue that although we cannot count on Chaucer's contemporary audience perceiving the intention and that *only*, there is more than a fair chance that they will have shared some of the basic assumptions of his text and responded to the closedness of textual direction. I do not share Knapp's admiration for 'the radical openness of language and textuality' in deconstructivist analysis, but admit for her convenient solution of having 'the historical conditions work to close them'.[20] The question is, however, whether medieval discourse was ever radically open in the first place, or whether this is just the case in principle, or in other words only in modern deconstructionist theoretical jargon.

Traugott Lawler uses an analysis of *The Squire's Tale* to reach a similar verdict. Lawler shows how Chaucer's intentionality is marked by an overall purpose to offer closed readings. Lawler's conclusion, which I will make my own, sharply sums up the difference between a very medieval and a very modern theory:

> In short, where Chaucer parts company with Derrida is in his willingness to give us narratives of presence and closure: in place of the deconstructionist's skepticism, he offers us faith.[21]

It should be added that Lawler sees Christian faith and patience to be the ultimate instructive purpose of *The Squire's Tale,* as well as a number of the other *Canterbury Tales.* The failure of deconstructionist criticism lies in its 'skepticism and distrust' of instructive purposes, according to Lawler.

This does not mean that we have to discard all modern theory of narrative. Deconstruction may not offer the most convincing perspective on Chaucer, but it is part of a modern theoretical apparatus and part of a general tendency in this century to combine linguistics with literary theory and criticism, a tendency headed by structuralism and semiotics. From this treasure of methodology medievalists have already borrowed extensively, and I would assume that this is very much the future for medieval studies. In this connection should also be mentioned the theories of literary communication that have been developed over the last few decades. Examples worth considering in relation to Chaucer's communication are Morton W. Bloomfield and Florence Ridley's papers in the already quoted *New Perspectives in Criticism.*

In her response to Bloomfield, Florence Ridley eloquently paraphrases Daniel Poiron and offers a literary communication model which shows how the text cannot be viewed in isolation:

> ... the text speaks (but the author assigned its speech), the genre shapes (but does not determine) the work, the cultural milieu effects (but does not fully account for) the creation, and the audience reception of whatever time and place brings the work to life.[22]

This is a fine process-oriented model, which describes the transmission of a text. However, some further specification is required. On the basis of French structuralism (mainly Barthes, Todorov, Genette) and the work of Wayne C. Booth, the literary theorist Seymour Chatman has developed a narrative communication model which distinguishes three different personages at the sending as well as the receiving end: the real author, the implied author, the narrator, the narratee, the implied audience, the real audience.[23] The distinctions made here are central to my perspective and will be employed to determine a basis for Chaucer's communication in *The Knight's Tale*. I shall therefore briefly sketch a definition based on Chatman's discussion, but for the purpose of the present study exemplified by using Chaucer's text as a model.

The real author, Chaucer, is the personage that we in principle, and in this case in practice, know little about, and who remains aloof from the text, ie he cannot be precisely reconstructed on the basis of it. For all we know he may have been bored, committed, serious, sarcastic, but all this is in a sense irrelevant for the communication, because here it is his relation with the product, the text as we have it, that counts. What we can try to reconstruct is the implied author, the personage who appears 'behind' the narrator, and who is the author's 'second self' (cf Chatman, p 148). Unlike the narrator he cannot tell us anything, but he is still the presence behind what is being said. That he is not identical with the real author is clear from the fact that one author can have different implied authors in different works. Let us consider Chatman's example:

> Not merely the narrator but the whole design of *Joseph Andrews* functions in a tone quite different from that of *Jonathan Wild* or *Amelia*. Henry Fielding created three clearly different implied authors.
> (p 148)

We may easily substitute works by Chaucer, say *The Book of the Duchess*, *Troilus and Criseyde* and *The Knight's Tale,* and reach a similar conclusion. The implied author is of course still a 'version' of Chaucer the real author, and so we may conveniently talk of for example Chaucer's voice or Chaucer's presence in relation to each work.

The narrator is in Chatman's book an optional personage, but he allows for the possibility of always recognizing a narrator, even though he or she may be close to or almost identical with the presence of the implied author, as in much of Chaucer's poetry. I shall take that option, since I assume that there is always a voice 'telling us' something, and the implied author cannot tell us anything; he is a presence behind. The most obvious type of narrator is of course the persona, often unreliable and certainly with a different perspective than the implied author. Such narrators we find among Chaucer's Canterbury pilgrims, although we cannot count on sustained persona-narration in *The Canterbury Tales*.[23]

The difference between narratee and implied audience can also be made with reference to the *Tales*: the pilgrims are the narratees, present in the literary work, whereas the implied audience are those that the tales were written for, whether a court circle or a wider audience. Finally the real audience are those that actually read or listen to the tales.

Chatman and other theorists of narrative in this century have been accused of being oriented almost exclusively towards the novel, and whereas there is undoubtedly some truth in that, at least Chatman's general model is directly applicable to Chaucer. Clare Regan Kinney, who has this protest against Chatman and his fellow theorists, sets out to create a theoretical apparatus specifically for poetic narrative.[24] She certainly succeeds in adding some significant perspectives on Chaucer's narrative poetry, asking basically how poetic form affects the narrative element. That this is no simple matter is acknowledged by herself:

> The perceived tension in a poetic fiction between its local schemes of elaboration and recapitulation and the more linear thrust of its discursive structure makes it the harder to apprehend such a work simultaneously as poem *and* narrative.
> (Kinney, pp 7–8)

Kinney's excellent reading of *Troilus and Criseyde* shows that such an apprehension *is* fortunately possible, and it will be my personal endeavour to reach a similar balance of perception of the inseparable poetic and narrative elements in *The Knight's Tale*.

# Notes to chapter 1

1. William Wordsworth, 'Letter to Walter Scott', November 7th, 1805. Ernest de Selincourt, ed., *Early Letters of William & Dorothy Wordsworth, 1787–1805* (Oxford: At the Clarendon Press, 1935), p 541. Wordsworth is comparing Chaucer's *Palamon and Arcite* (*The Knight's Tale*) with Dryden's translation.

2. William Blake, *A Descriptive Catalogue*, number 3, 'Sir Jeffery Chaucer and the nine and twenty Pilgrims on their journey to Canterbury', London, 1809, p 114. Extract repr. in Malcolm Andrew, ed., *Critical Essays on Chaucer's Canterbury Tales* (Milton Keynes: Open University Press, 1991).

3. A representative selection of historical Chaucer criticism can be found in D. S. Brewer, ed., *Chaucer: The Critical Heritage, I–II* (London: Routledge & Kegan Paul, 1978). The Blake quotation above appears in I, p 252, whereas the Wordsworth quotation is not included.

4. For a fuller discussion of the history of Chaucer criticism see Alcuin Blamires, *The Canterbury Tales: The Critics Debate* (Houndsmill and London: MacMillan, 1987). A more generalized survey of modern Chaucer criticism can be found in my article 'Chaucer and Modern Criticism'. *(Engelsk Meddelelser*, 1993).

5. G. L. Kittredge, 'Chaucer's Discussion of Marriage' in *Modern Philology*, 9, 1912, 435. Also reprinted in Andrew, p 2.

6. The fullest statement of the dramatic theory is R. M. Lumiansky, *Of Sondry Folk: The Dramatic Principle in the Canterbury Tales* (Austin: University of Texas Press, 1955, repr. 1980). For some less 'dramatic' views of coherence between the tales see Helen Cooper, *The Structure of the Canterbury Tales* (Athens: University of Georgia Press and London: Duckworth, 1983) and Jerome Mandel, *Geoffrey Chaucer: Building the Fragments of the Canterbury Tales* (London and Toronto: Associated University Press, 1992).

7. E. Talbot Donaldson, 'Chaucer the Pilgrim' in *Speaking of Chaucer* (London: The Athlone Press, University of London, 1970), pp 1–12. Also repr. in Andrew, pp 67–75.

8. Charles Muscatine, 'Form, Texture and Meaning in Chaucer's *Knight's Tale*' in *Publications of the Modern Language Association of America*, LXV, 1950. Also repr. in Edward Wagenknecht, ed., *Chaucer: Modern Essays in Criticism* (New York: Oxford University Press, 1959). The quotation appears on p 69.

9. Charles Muscatine, *Chaucer and the French Tradition: A Study in Style and Meaning* (Berkeley and L. A.: University of California Press, 1957), pp 171–2. This book also comprises a revised version of the article above.

10. Ralph Baldwin, *The Unity of the Canterbury Tales* (*Anglistica 5*; Copenhagen: Rosenkilde & Bagger, 1955), pp 67 and 77.

11. D. W. Robertson, *A Preface to Chaucer* (Princeton: Princeton University Press, 1962).

12. David Aers, *Chaucer, Langland, and the Creative Imagination* (London: Routledge and Kegan Paul, 1980) and 'Criseyde: Woman in Medieval Society' in *The Chaucer Review*, 13, 1979.

13. Alistair Minnis, 'Chaucer and Comtemporary Literary Theory' in D. Rose, ed., *New Perspectives in Chaucer Criticism* (Oklohoma: Pilgrim Books, 1981), pp 56–7 and Alistair Minnis, *Medieval Theories of Authorship: Scholastic Literary Attitudes in the Later Middle Ages* (London: Scholar Press, 1984).

14. Blamires, pp 50–1.

15. In a recent article, 'Poet & Persona; Writing the Reader in *Troilus*' in *Papers presented to Andreas Haarder; Pre-Publications of the English Department of Odense University*, 1994, Marianne Børch has questioned this assumption, based on her reading of the first manuscript version of this book. She states that the 'narrative contract' is 'insufficiently

established, if indeed its principal basis is the *disclaimer* of responsibility in *ProlMill.*' (Børch, p. 58) I leave the issue for the reader to decide, yet maintain my stand, because I find a disclaimer the best possible proof of the existence of an understood agreement about narrative transmission. See further the discussion of narrative contracts in chapter 4.

16. The case can be made also for many of Chaucer's earlier works. For a fine analysis of narratorial presence in Chaucer's early poems see Angus A. Somerville, *Chaucer's Treatment of the Narrator and a Comparative Study of Other Medieval Texts* (unpublished Ph. D.-thesis, Glasgow University, 1969).
17. Derek Pearsall, *The Life of Geoffrey Chaucer* (Oxford: Blackwell, 1992), pp 185–90 and 151–9. Pearsall opts for an original date for 'Palamon and Arcite' around 1381–2, but allows for the obvious revisions to fit *The Canterbury Tales*. I accept this dating as the most convincing, well aware that some scholars have argued otherwise.
18. Winthrop Wetherbee, 'Convention and Authority: A Comment on Some Critical Approaches to Chaucer' in Rose, especially p 80.
19. Peggy A. Knapp, 'Deconstructing *The Canterbury Tales:* pro' and Traugott Lawler, 'Deconstructing *The Canterbury Tales:* con' in *Studies in the Age of Chaucer*, 9, 1987. Both repr. in Andrews.
20. Knapp, especially 74–75 and 80.
21. Lawler, 90.
22. Morton W. Bloomfield, 'Contemporary Literary Theory and Chaucer' and Florence Ridley, 'A Response to "Contemporary Literary Theory and Chaucer"', both in D. Rose, ed., *New Perspectives in Chaucer Criticism* (Oklahoma: Pilgrim Books, 1981). The quotation is from p 49.
23. Seymour Chatman, *Story and Discourse: Narrative Structure in Fiction and Film* (Ithaca and London: Cornell University Press, 1978). See especially chapters four and five.
24. Clare Regan Kinney, *Strategies of Poetic Narrative: Chaucer, Spenser, Milton, Eliot* (Cambridge: Cambridge University Press, 1992), especially p 4.

# CHAPTER 2

# The Knight's Tale: Narrator and Narration

In the maze of criticism commenting on *The Knight's Tale*, the student might soon feel at a loss. In two modern introductions, summing up on evidence from analysis of the narrator's role, we find the statements that 'the "I" of narration is demonstrably not the I of the ostensible teller [ie the Knight]' (David Lawton), and that 'Chaucer remains to a large extent invisible' (Michael Alexander). Taken in combination these interpretations seem to leave us with nobody to tell the tale, perhaps a medieval version of the famous deconstructionist death of the author?[1] Other Chaucer introductions (by Peggy Knapp and Derek Brewer respectively) are equally confusing for the student in insisting either that 'the Knight's narrative techniques dominate the tale' or that 'there is no doubt it is Chaucer [who tells the poem].'[2] In this chapter I will explore the critical stances on narration in *The Knight's Tale* in more nuanced detail and offer some clarification of the opposing views and concepts.

The rather extreme formulation by Brewer above seems to break a basic rule given by handbooks on literary analysis and teachers of literature alike: Never assume identity between author and narrator. That this is in fact what Brewer wants us to do becomes clear in a reinforcement of the point, taken from a more recent publication:

> Nor is there any so-called Narrator, different from the poet-as-storyteller. The presence of a Narrator must always imply a self-conscious irony indicated within the text. There is no evidence of this kind in *The Reeve's Tale* (indeed there is far less evidence for it in most of Chaucer's poetry than most modern critics seem to believe).[3]

It appears that the 'poet-as-storyteller' is identified with the author, and that Brewer here uses 'Narrator' in the sense of 'persona'. And since, according to Brewer, there is no persona in *The Knight's Tale* (*Chaucer: An Introduction,* p 112), the narrator becomes also the author, Chaucer. Unnecessary terminological confusion, as it seems, even though Chatman's invitation to count a narrator as optional may lend some support to Brewer's case. Disregarding the vague terminology, Brewer's view is an important one, which finds support in other prominent criticism, reacting against a modern tendency to see *personae* and irony everywhere in Chaucer. Derek Pearsall, perhaps, launches the strongest attack on such a tendency in his Chaucer biography:

> The "Chaucerian persona" has had a particularly vigorous critical life, offering an opportunity for interpreters to substitute almost anyone they want for the unnamable prime suspect. Such interpretations masquerade as an open-minded approach to the text, one that does not want to identify a single intentionality in the person of the author, but what they more often do is to substitute for the enigmatic or elusive intentions of the author the only too obvious intentions of the critic. The cult of the persona has thus become a technique for systematically ironizing the text and appropriating it to the service of particular kinds of programmatic interpretation. Some of the results have been very strange.[4]

It should be said that the context is different, a discussion of *The Book of the Duchess*, and that Pearsall operates with a narrator-author identification only in Chaucer's poetry before *The Canterbury Tales*, but the attack on the persona is clear enough. Specifically on *The Knight's Tale*, which, as mentioned in chapter one, he counts as a close adaption of the earlier story of 'Palamon and Arcite' and thus also as pre-*Canterbury Tales*, Pearsall has written:

> Beyond this obvious congruence of tale and teller, however, it would be unwise to go. We know nothing of the Knight's "character", and there is nothing in the telling of the tale to induce us to believe that it is intended to express the point of view or feelings or ideas of a particular "character".[5]

Pearsall is warning specifically against automatic character application of the portrait from the *General Prologue*, emphasizing here, as elsewhere, that there is *not* in *The Canterbury Tales* any obvious link between direct characterization in the *General Prologue* and indirect characterization in the tale. In this he is on a par with Lawton, quoted above, who specifies that the Knight only speaks in his character's voice at the beginning of the tale (859–92) and 'awakes as from a long sleep' only in the very last line of his tale.[6] The kind of inconsistency of narratorial voice that is indicated by this approach is lent support also by David Aers:

> As throughout the *Canterbury Tales* there is simply no hard-and-fast rule about the relations between author, fictional tellers and tales, nor is there always a consistent narrative voice in even one tale. It is important that the reader neither seeks nor imposes the kind of "coherence" here that Chaucer's texts seem quite uninterested in.[7]

If we connect this statement with my discussion in chapter one, it will be clear that Aers (like Brewer, Pearsall and Lawton) is reacting against the critical trend of operating with a persona-pilgrim-narrator sparked off by Donaldson's article 'Chaucer the Pilgrim', but ultimately deriving from Kittredge's 'dramatic' reading. The reaction to such readings of *The Knight's Tale* would perhaps have been less sharp if the 'chivalric' teller-tale relationship traditionally invoked in it had not been seriously challenged by Terry Jones, who in 1979 with his controversial book *Chaucer's Knight* provoked some critical response that has thrown new light on the tale's narration. Whereas Jones' view of the Knight as a cold-blooded mercenary captain, a professional killer, who is ironically revealed through the narration of his tale, has been once and for all refuted, various dramatic or ironic readings of the Knight's role as narrator have in fact been offered in 1980s and 90s criticism.[8]

It would in fact be fair to say that the dominant modes of Chaucer criticism even after the Jones controversy have failed to answer to the important reservations put forward by for example Pearsall, Aers and Lawton. A very brief case study of some recent Chaucer criticism will illustrate my point.

The view put forth by Olsson that 'a pastiche of a knight ... creates a pastiche of tale' in fact strongly echoes Terry Jones, although based on a reading of the Knight's character as an all too benevolent, old-fashioned advocate of chivalry. Like Jones, Olsson gets the problem passages of the tale resolved by having them reflect the Knight's shortcomings and single-minded perspective. This goes especially for the handling of Boethian philosophy in the poem, and on this point Olsson agrees with Schweitzer, who argues that the philosophical material is 'much beyond the Knight's comprehension'.[9] A complicated discussion, which I shall return to later, but suffice it to say here that the poor persona-Knight in these interpretations comes to carry a lot of responsibility on his shoulders, including an unsatisfactory story-line and uneven poetry, although all this is, admittedly, compensated for by the irony of the author behind him.

Extreme, persona-based perceptions of the narration leading to innumerable ironies can also be found in the reading of F. Anne Payne. According to Payne, the Knight is literally the composer, who has his own narrative technique, even selects from the *Teseida* and in general remains in control.[10] It appears that Chaucer has lost all responsibility for his work. This only as an illustration of what the persona-concept may lead on to, and Payne is by no means the only critic to have confused the concepts of author and narrator, as we have seen already.

Peggy Knapp, who is an advocate of New Historicism, sees *The Knight's Tale* as reflecting its teller's discourse, belonging to the second estate. She fully endorses the persona-based 'character' perspective on the Knight, as suggested by the quotation at the beginning of this chapter, and in fact Knapp focuses so much on the narrator that the reader is encouraged to see the tale as primarily being *about* the Knight. Thus also such subheadings as 'The Knight himself' and 'The Discourse of Nobility' in a chapter called 'Chivalry and its Discontents.'[11] This appears to be a far more wide-reaching attack on traditional approaches than Olsson's and Payne's, since the tale's primary interest derives from the persona, who becomes the hub of the wheel, not unlike Jones' Knight. And so in turn the tale is also reduced to an 'aristocratic chronicle' (p 30), a far cry from wideranging generic modes such as romance, epic or tragedy, with which the tale has traditionally been labelled.

This particular kind of reductionism is important to consider, since it appears in the works of other New Historicists as well. Thus according to Stephen Knight, what we have is 'an archetypal, romance-like presentation of the world from the viewpoint of cavalry through the mouthpiece of chivalry;' and Chaucerian texts, we learn, are best read 'in terms of social and historical meaning and function.'[12] Again this focuses so entirely on knighthood and chivalry that other aspects of the tale, notably aesthetic, poetic and narrative effects, are disregarded.

Another New Historicist, Lee Patterson, like Stephen Knight bases almost his entire study of *The Knight's Tale* on text-external evidence. Some twenty pages of a fiftyfive-page chapter on the tale are in fact devoted to the famous Scrope-Grosvenor dispute about the right to bear certain arms, a court case from which we have one single record of Chaucer giving evidence. This case story is used in support of Patterson's view of 'the Crisis of Chivalric Identity' (chapter heading), a discussion of historical evidence occupying another ten pages.[13] Such a reading may leave us with enlightened understanding of chivalry, but the connection to Chaucer and *The Knight's Tale*, being based on such loose evidence, is never made convincing. Probably because the few records on Chaucer we have on the point of chivalry suggest not his distaste or detachment from, but his acceptance of the existence of chivalry. We must not forget that Chaucer helped organise Richard II's tournament at Smithfield. And as for his statement in the Scrope-Grosvenor dispute, all he does is give support for Scrope, based on a personal recollection of having known Scrope using the coat-of-arms first. There is no evidence of Chaucer having felt any disgust or even remote antipathy in connection with the case as such and with chivalry in general.[14]

However, Patterson has got something to say on the tale itself and its narration. First, in a general introduction, he endorses the persona-oriented interpretation of the text being about its speaker, on the basis of a quotation from Marshall Leicester about the *Canterbury Tales* generally. Patterson adds that 'the very form of the *Tales* always raises the possibility of a radically subjectivized discourse' and also claims that the pilgrims often 'appropriate the narratorial voice'.[15] Whereas this is easy to follow in Patterson's fine analyses from *The General Prologue* and could be extended to include the subjectivized discourse in the prologues of the Wife of Bath and the Pardoner, the claim is more problematic for the rest of the *Canterbury Tales* and for *The Knight's Tale* in particular. It is indeed curious that Patterson should recognize 'the rigorously conventional and objectified opening trio of Knight, Squire and Yeoman' (p 29), and then base an interpretation of *The Knight's Tale* on the Knight as a persona. The explanation lies perhaps in Marshall Leicester's idea of 'the pilgrims as the products rather than as the producers of their tales.'[16] Ie we have an 'objectified' Knight in the *General Prologue*, who becomes subjectified in his tale. Or perhaps the explanation is that the Knight-persona in his tale represents an embodiment of 'the collective consciousness of the second estate', as Patterson has it (p 169, and cf Peggy Knapp, above), ie a pastiche of a knight in Olsson's terms? In this way the Knight acquires the status of a depersonalized persona. Patterson's view of *The Knight's Tale* is summed up in a brief passage, p 244:

> The *Knight's Tale* represents in its narrative and exemplifies by its mode of narration the crisis of governance experienced by the fourteenth-century aristocracy.

My own analysis will illustrate how much I disagree, but at this stage may I remind the reader of the quotation from Derek Pearsall above (p 30) about persona, ironizing the text, appropriating and programmatic interpretation.

The *Knight's Tale* is not about the Knight, I have argued, but this is not to say that we should accept the other extreme, that the speaker is Chaucer, at least in Brewer's unmodified sense. And obviously some of the many critics who operate with a persona have been able to demonstrate mechanisms of narratorial involvement which characterize the overall voice. Winthrop Wetherbee sees the Knight as 'at once the instigator of the tale and an enthusiastic member of the audience, unquestioning of the values of his protagonists,' suggesting the sort of narratorial stance described by critics in the general narrator ('Chaucer the pilgrim'), but then adds significantly, to characterize a development in the fatal tournament scene, that we have here 'an insider addressing an audience of aficionados.'[17] This would in fact suggest a difference from the outsider-status of the Chaucer-character in the General Prologue and the links (eg VII, 695–706). A point well worth considering. Wetherbee also, as do several others critics, establishes a connection between the Knight and Theseus (p 40). Barbara Nolan has suggested that the link is based on 'Stoic values' and J. A. Burrow that it is apparent in the use of language, again valuable observations, which will be considered further in later chapters.[18]

So the persona-concept, if not taken too literally, can lead to fruitful results. And basically there *is* of course a Knight present, whether or not he is only a framing device. Even that has its effect, as noted by A. C. Spearing:

> We do not know what changes Chaucer may have made in this separate work when he included it in *The Canterbury Tales*; but even if he did not alter a word, "the love of Palamon and Arcite" was inevitably transformed into a different poem when it became *The Knight's Tale*. The effect on any tale of giving it a fictional teller and setting it in the context of a pilgrimage where the other pilgrims also tell tales of quite different kinds will be to place it in an entirely new perspective.[19]

The perspective of the other *Canterbury Tales* should indeed be remembered, for example when we see the Miller wanting to 'quite' *The Knight's Tale* (I, 3119). And as far as voice is concerned, *The Knight's Tale* represents one of *many* styles mastered by Chaucer (cf the discussion in chapter one). That it is complicated and uneven will appear from my analysis, but finally in this chapter let us consider some possible solutions for avoiding the pitfalls connected with the persona-concept on the one hand, and avoiding a complete author-narrator identification on the other.

Marshall Leicester invents a 'Leicester's razor' to suggest that only one speaker is necessary, and that Chaucer as this speaker impersonates a number of characters (pilgrims). This is intended to spell out the difference between *voice* (= speaker impersonated) and *presence* behind (= Chaucer). Indeed a practical and simple solution, but the complications of changing voices within one tale (cf Aers, quoted above, p 31) are not easily accounted for, as Leicester's attempt to analyse the narration of *The Knight's Tale* shows. We are left with both an extremely vaguely defined speaker *and* voice, the latter disconcertingly referred to as simply – the Knight.[20]

Three studies from the eighties take the conceptual discussion to a far more satisfactory conclusion. Leicester does not in essence get beyond the dramatic theory, although he opens the path, but C. David Benson, David Lawton, and Leonard M. Koff, in respectively *Chaucer's Drama of Style: Poetic Variety and Contrast in the Canterbury Tales, Chaucer's Narrators,* and *Chaucer and the Art of Storytelling* together set a different agenda in focusing less on pilgrim characters than on the techniques of poetic narrative (cf also Kinney, discussed in chapter 1). How difficult this can be is illustrated by Benson's scruples about choosing appropriate terms for avoiding the persona:

> Awkward as it undoubtedly is, I sometimes choose the word "poet," rather than the more natural "voice" or "teller" in a deliberate attempt to depersonalize my analysis and prevent the reader from thinking of the pilgrim instead of the tale.[21]

In fact this choice allows Benson to focus on features of *the text itself* and carry out an excellent analysis of modes of narration in *The Knight's Tale* and *The Miller's Tale,* for instance structure, characterization, word choice, imagery and speech (p 67).

'Poet' and 'poetics' may be too unfamiliar terms in this context, so

perhaps Lawton's solution is preferable, although he is very much on a par
with Benson. In a discussion of Bakhtin's *heteroglossia* Lawton finds this
term inadequate in connection with Chaucer, because it fails to distinguish
between Chaucer's and the pilgrim's voices:

> We are left not with a speaker but with a tone.
> Yet this tone is not single or unitary. It is a complex and multiple
> play of voices. All of these voices are equally alienated from their
> ostensible, presumed or possible source. They are apocryphal
> voices.'[22]

The 'tone' as composed by several 'voices', sometimes 'apocryphal', i. e.
unreliable or removed from Chaucer; handy literary tools for working
with *The Canterbury Tales*. As are the 'open' and 'closed' persona distinctions also suggested by Lawton (eg *The Pardoner's Tale* being open and
*The Pardoner's Prologue* closed; Lawton's example, p 7), that is if we want to
operate with *personae* at all. Lawton grudgingly accepts the persona, because the concept helps correct the trap of interpreting directly 'what
Chaucer thought,' yet he says:

> ... the real demerit of persona-oriented criticism is that it diverts
> attention from language and styles into a reckoning that is dramatic
> and psychological. Questions about tone are therefore referred in the
> wrong direction.[23]

Lawton is expressing a sentiment very close to that of Dieter Mehl, quoted
in my introduction, but he has gone further than Mehl and speaks from a
critical vantage point some twenty years later. His suggestions for a focus
on language and styles, and his concepts of tone, voice and open/closed
persona-narration in Chaucer can be easily combined with Chatman's and
Kinney's narrative theories and approach. Thus a theoretical, and terminological framework is beginning to take form.

My final terminological modification is based on Koff's study and is
concerned with voice. In his introduction Koff states that 'Chaucer's text
has a voice everywhere', and later this is exemplified by for instance a
reading of *The Pardoner's Tale* as characterized by a complex voice resulting
from Chaucer's 'bemused and endearing' presence as storyteller combined
with the Pardoner's 'menacing and parasitic' position.[24] In this and other
examples Koff shows how it is possible in general terms to characterize the

elements of poetic performance by distinguishing marked attitudinal stances of voice. That this is no longer so simple when we analyse in detail is another matter, and, failing to come up with any satisfactory solution in *The Knight's Tale*, Koff in fact takes refuge in a simplified conclusion: '*The Knight's Tale* is not problematic. It is only incomplete' (p. 182).

Agreeing that Chaucer's text indeed has voice everywhere, my challenge will be to show that no simple generalization about narrative voice in *The Knight's Tale* is valid. On the contrary, the voice is highly problematic: changing, nuanced and sometimes deceptive. And the tale *is* complete in as far as Chaucer has managed to form an artistic unity out of great stylistic complexity.

## Notes to chapter 2

1. David Lawton, *Chaucer's Narrators* (Cambridge: D. S. Brewer, 1985), p 96, and Michael Alexander, *York Notes on* The Knight's Tale. *Geoffrey Chaucer* (London: Longman, 1981, 2nd impression, 1990), p 87. Cf also Lawton, p xiv. For a discussion of 'the death of the author' see Derek Pearsall, *The Life of Geoffrey Chaucer* (Oxford: Blackwell, 1992), pp 3–4.
2. Peggy Knapp, *Chaucer and the Social Contest* (New York and London: Routledge, 1990), p 19 and Derek Brewer, *Chaucer: An Introduction.* (London: Longman, 1984), p 112.
3. Derek Brewer, 'The Reeve's Tale' in J. O. Fichte, ed., *Chaucer's Frame Tales: The Physical and Metaphysical* (Tübingen: Günter Narr Verlag & Cambridge: D. S. Brewer, 1987), p 81.
4. Derek Pearsall, p 86.
5. Derek Pearsall, *The Canterbury Tales.* (London: Allen and Unwin, 1985), p 116.
6. Lawton, p 96.
7. David Aers, *Chaucer* (Brighton: The Harvester Press, 1986), p 71.
8. Terry Jones, *Chaucer's Knight* (London: Eyre Methuen, 1980). The points against Jones are made by notably Maurice Keen, 'Chaucer's Knight, the English Aristocracy and the Crusade' in Scattergood and Sherbourne, eds., *English Court Culture in the Later Middle Ages* (London: Duckworth, 1983), pp 45–61 and in David Aers' review of Jones' book in *Studies in the Age of Chaucer*, 4, 1982, 169–75. See also John H. Pratt, 'Was Chaucer's Knight Really a Mercenary?' in *The Chaucer Review*, 22, 1, 1987, 8–27, R. F. Yeager, 'Pax Poetica: On the Pacifism of Chaucer and Gower' in *Studies in the Age of Chaucer*, 20, 9, 1987, 97–121 and D. W. Robertson Jr., 'The Probable Date and Purpose of Chaucer's *Knight's Tale*' in *Studies in Philology, 84, 1987,* 418–40.
9. Kurt Olsson, '*Securitas* and Chaucer's Knight' in *Studies in the Age of Chaucer*, 9, 1987, 123–53. Edward C. Schweitzer, 'Fate and Freedom in the *Knight's Tale*' in *Studies in the Age of Chaucer*, 3, 1981, 13–45.
10. F. Anne Payne, *Chaucer and Menippean Satire* (Wisconsin: The University of Wisconsin Press, 1981). See especially p 233 and p 235.
11. Peggy Knapp, part I, chapter 2.
12. Stephen Knight, *Geoffrey Chaucer* (Oxford: Blackwell, 1986), p 83 and p 6.

13. Lee Patterson, *Chaucer and the Subject of History* (London: Routledge, 1991), chapter 3.
14. Derek Pearsall, *The Life of Geoffrey Chaucer*, especially pp 9–11 and Crow & Olson, eds., *Chaucer Life Records* (Oxford: Clarendon Press, 1966), chapter eighteen, especially pp 370–1.
15. Patterson, pp 27–8.
16. H. Marshall Leicester Jr., 'The Art of Impersonation: A General Prologue to the *Canterbury Tales*' in *Publications of the Modern Language Association of America*, 95, 1980, 218. Also repr. in Malcolm Andrew, ed., *Critical Essays on Chaucer's Canterbury Tales* (Milton Keynes: Open University Press, 1991), pp 138–54.
17. Winthrop Wetherbee, *Chaucer: The Canterbury Tales* (Cambridge: Cambridge University Press, 1989), p 41.
18. Barbara Nolan, *Chaucer and the Tradition of the Roman Antique* (Cambridge: *Cambridge Studies in Medieval Literature*, 15, 1992), p 251 and J. A. Burrow 'Chaucer's *Knight's Tale* and the Three Ages of Man' in Burrow, ed., *Essays on Medieval Literature* (Oxford: Clarendon Press, 1984), pp 46–7.
19. A. C. Spearing, ed., *The Knight's Tale* (Cambridge: Cambridge University Press, 1966), p 47. Spearing has informed me that a forthcoming revision of this edition will do away with the persona-narrator entirely, but the point made here is of course still valid.
20. Leicester, esp. 215, 218 and 220. Leicester's article was written as a response to Donald R. Howard, *The Idea of the Canterbury Tales* (Berkeley: University of California Press, 1976), especially p 264 ff. For an apt comment on the inadequacy of both approaches see also Alcuin Blamires, *The Canterbury Tales: The Critics Debate*. (Houndmills and London: Macmillan, 1987), pp 39–40 and Barbara Nolan's response to Leicester, '"A Poet Ther Was": Chaucer's Voices in the General Prologue to *The Canterbury Tales*' in *Publications of the Modern Language Association of America*, 101, 1986.
21. C. David Benson, *Chaucer's Drama of Style: Poetic Variety and Contrast in the Canterbury Tales* (Chapelhill and London: The University of North Carolina Press, 1986), p 21.
22. Lawton, p 4.
23. Lawton, p 7.
24. Leonard M. Koff, *Chaucer and the Art of Storytelling* (Berkeley & L. A., University of California Press, 1988), pp 4 and 173. On a par with Koff, Ronald B Herzman has stated that 'the voice is ultimately always Chaucer's', explaining that 'Chaucer's is the voice which controls the voices of the characters in the tales.' See Herzman, 'The Paradox of Form: *The Knight's Tale* and Chaucerian Aesthetics' in *Papers on Language and Literature*, 10, 1974, also repr. in Willi Erzgräber, ed., *Geoffrey Chaucer* (Darmstadt: Wissenschaftliche Buchgesellschaft, 1983).

# CHAPTER 3

# Chaucer's Shape-Shifting of his Text: Poetic Design And Narrative Strategy

The assumption that Chaucer's voice is everywhere, combined with my earlier analysis of his authorial role, points to a recognition that he is at all levels responsible for poetic design and narrative strategy. In this connection the question so often posed in criticism of what Chaucer *did to* his main source is dangerously inaccurate, since it suggests by implication that the source *directs* the artistic effort. Let me stress that the source should only be regarded as the raw material, and that the process of artistic recreation involves complete shape-shifting of the text.[1]

In the introduction to his 1966 edition of *The Knight's Tale* A. C. Spearing goes against excessive concern with the sources on the grounds that this may distract attention from the poem itself.[2] Such a New Critical emphasis indeed has some validity as a warning to overzealous practitioners of source study, who still today come up with fanciful suggestions about what Chaucer will have read or known.[3] However, as Elisabeth Salter already showed in 1962, it can be highly enlightening to consider *The Knight's Tale* in a comparative analysis with its main source, Boccaccio's *Teseida*, because this allows an insight into the process of artistic innovation and a perspective on how far Chaucer's poetry is anchored in tradition, whether Italian, French, classical – or English.[4]

A thorough study of the influence of classical epic, mainly Statius' *Thebaid*, which Chaucer knew, is David Anderson's *Before The Knight's Tale: Imitation of Classical Epic in Boccaccio's Teseida*. Anderson demonstrates how the reshaping of the epic from Boccaccio's twelve books to Chaucer's four, with the reduction of lines from nearly 10,000 to 2250, still allows Chaucer to operate with a familiar epic form, the *metrum heroicum*, in the tradition of some of Chaucer's favourite classical writers, Virgil, Lucan, and Statius himself.[5] As noted by F. Anne Payne, the reduction of lines is matched by a narrowing of action to three selected years from Boccaccio's timespan of ten years.[6] The storyline is reduced to its bare essentials, and most of the longwinded descriptions in *Il Teseida*, notably the war scenes in book I and II and the lists for the tournament in book VI, have been cut out or replaced by summarizing passages. The chief additions of material are the philosophical passages adapted from Boethius' *De Consolatione Philosophiae* (translated by Chaucer and referred to by him as *Boece*), and many descriptive passages that are retained have been significantly re-shaped, including the descriptions of Venus and Mars in Theseus' amphitheatre, a more detailed consideration of which will be undertaken later.

Innumerable studies have accounted minutely for the exact correspondences between Chaucer's and Boccaccio's versions, and of course Chaucer is highly indebted to both Boccaccio and his Italian tradition. However, as an important modern contributor to the comparative approach, Piero Boitani, has pointed out, the *Teseida* is only 'a starting point, a tableau on which Chaucer elaborates' and 'the ultimate difference between *Teseida* and *Knight's Tale* is one of narrative method and imagination.'[7] A brief comparison of narrative stance in the two poems will confirm this point.

E che ella da me per voi sia compilata, due cose fra l'altre il manifestano. L'una si è che ció che sotto il nome dell'uno de' due amanti e della giovane amata si conta essere stato, ricordandovi bene, e io a voi di me e voi a me di voi, se non mentiste, potreste conoscere essere stato detto e fatto in parte: quale de' due si sia non discuopro, ché so che ve ne avvedrete.

And two features among others make it plain that I have composed this for your sake. One is that what the story relates concerning one of the two lovers and the young woman he loves may be taken by you, if you well recall and were sincere, to correspond to what was said and done by both of us, I shall not reveal which of the two I mean, for I am sure you will know.[8]

Thus Boccaccio-as-poet addresses his 'Fiametta' in a prologue to his *Teseida,* outspokenly involving his personal experience of love in it. Further on in this initial dedication, Boccaccio even ventures to suggest that his poem might cause his beloved Fiametta to change her mind and take him back as a lover. This stance and tone is quite characteristic for *The Teseida*, marked by grand epic style and passionate romance, and including often highflown language. The narratorial voice sides with the lovers and their endeavour to come to terms with the impossible love triangle. For

instance Emilia is given a very sympathetic treatment and also an active
part in accepting the initial outcome of Arcita's and Palemone's battle for
her:

> Or ha preso partito e appagata
> dagl'iddii tiensi d'avere il migliore;
> e già d'Arcita si dice sposata,
> e già li porta non usato amore
> occultamente, e già spessa fiata
> priega l'iddii per lo suo signore;
> e con nuovo disio il va mirando
> l'opere sue sopra tutte lodando.
> (*Il Teseida,* book 8, stanza 127)

> Now she has decided, and contented with the judgment of the gods
> she resolves to accept the better one. And she already thinks of
> herself as wedded to Arcita; already she secretly harbours an un-
> accustomed passion for him, and already she begs the gods again and
> again to let him be her husband. And she goes on looking at him
> with unwonted desire, admiring his conduct above all others.
> (N. Haveley, transl., p 138)

It will appear that Emilia is vastly different from Chaucer's Emily, often
noted for her passive character and lack of individual characterization. The
narratorial stance in *The Knight's Tale* is indeed altogether different from
that in the *Teseida,* since all characters, except Theseus, are reduced to
types, and since the narrator never involves himself on either side in the
love story. J. A. Burrow remarks that 'the narrator's attitude to the lovers
... is detached,' and Kathleen A. Blake has shown how the narrator refuses
to take sides, always presenting the *probleme d'amour* in terms of alterna-
tives, as in the often quoted direct address to the audience at the end of
book 1.[9]

It is all the more noteworthy that Chaucer chooses such a stance for his
narrator when we consider some of his other poems that incorporate love
stories. The narrator in *Troilus and Criseyde* stands out as deeply involved
with the fates of his lovers (cf chapter 1, p 17) and declares himself 'a
servant of the servants of the God of Love' (I, 15–16). In *The Clerk's Tale*,
the narrator steps in on behalf of patient Griselda (outspokenly in 76 ff, 457
and 620–22), and in *The Legend of Good Women* the narrator continually

sides with the women suffering in love. The ring of words like 'pitee' and 'routhe' will be familiar to all readers of these and many other works by Chaucer, alongside the 'joye' and 'gladnesse' from the times when love relationships strike a merrier note. It may be concluded that the narratorial stance in most of Chaucer's poems involving a love story is highly sympathetic towards lovers and love, and that the audience is continually invited to share that sympathy.

Not so in *The Knight's Tale*. There is a significant absence of narratorial comments on passionate love, and where any sympathy is evoked it is rarely for the lovers. Theseus shows 'pitee', 'compassioun', 'mercy' and 'grace' for the mourning widows and for the lovers in the episode outside the grove (920, 950, 953, 955, 1110, 1117, 1173, 1761, 1828, 1874), but the characteristic representations of the lovers involve rather their own complaints of 'wo', 'distresse', 'hevynesse' and 'smerte' (for instance 1229, 1296, 1298, 1392, 1453, 1456, 2841, 2847). And whereas both Palamon and Arcite *pray* for 'pitee', 'mercy' and 'routhe' in the temple scenes (1225, 2231, 2233, 2371, 2392, 2419), 'joye', 'gladnesse' and 'blisse' occur mainly in their negated forms (1229, 1250, 1271), except at the very end of the tale. This analysis points to a cruel universe of love, and indeed there is not a single tender love scene in *The Knight's Tale*, unless we want to count the episode surrounding Arcite's death as such. Only once (2345) does a narratorial comment directly express 'pitee', and that is for the almost anonymous Emily:

> But only for the feere thus hath she cried
> And weep that it was pitee for to heere.
> And therwithal Dyane gan appeere.
> (2341–3)

It has often been suggested that Theseus is an agent for the narrator's point of view, and certainly it is true that Theseus releases some pain by his actions and also that he provides a humorous relief. However, the tone concerning love remains to a large extent sombre and grave in spite of Theseus' efforts, and I believe that this is due to a narratorial stance aloof from Theseus as well as the lovers. The suffering in Arcite and Palamon's universe of love is underlined by a representational form in which the narrator *shows* their misery without *commenting* on it. Pathos is evoked by implication, not appealed for.

I have so far focused on the narratorial stance in relation to the love story and discussed the effects of the narrator's non-involvement. This is not the same as to postulate a general stance of distance, since *The Knight's Tale* is concerned with a much wider perspective than the *Teseida*. Whereas the *Teseida* has the love story as its central element, the focus in Chaucer's poem is shifted towards a philosophical angle on the pagan universe. As Spearing has rightly argued, the conventional *demande d'amour* at the end of book 1 is in a sense inappropriate, because the question is posed on a philosophical background rather than in medieval courtly terms.[10] It may be added that the tradition of courtly love is present in *The Knight's Tale*, but that the poetic design reduces it to mere stereotype, such as Arcite's conventional lovesickness at the beginning of book II (1355–79), which is impatiently interrupted by the narrator in line 1380: 'What sholde I al day of his wo endite?' Again there is no narratorial sympathy or involvement; only a desire to get on with the story and on to matters of real concern. Here as in general the narrative strategy consists chiefly of an attempt to suppress what Clare Regan Kinney has called 'goal-resistant narrative dilation' in favour of 'goal-determined narrative design.'[11]

Narratorial involvement occurs generally on two levels: Firstly, when the art of storytelling is concerned. As Jennifer Strauss points out *The Knight's Tale* has more markers of narratorial self-consciousness than any other of the *Tales*.[12] Secondly, whenever a narrative dilation is philosophical or symbolically illustrative of the poem's pagan universe. The foregrounding of philosophical and pagan subject matter and the narratorial self-consciousness will be analysed in more detail, but first let us consider in further general terms the discourse and structure that derive from the narrative stance and strategy.

Peggy Knapp and Stephen Knight, both operating with the Knight-persona as narrator, find the discourse respectively 'patriarchal' and 'literary and bookish', and similarly 'archaic' has been used to classify both the Knight and his tale.[13] The persona interpretation is of some importance here, since these elements are claimed to fit a knight who appears from the *General Prologue* to be widely experienced in matters of chivalry, and who clearly belongs to an old and well-merited generation of knighthood. However, old and experienced is hardly the same as archaic and I would strongly suggest that only the setting for the tale, not its narrative style, qualifies for this label. 'Literary and bookish' might be used about Chaucer's authorial interest in the sources, but the expression hardly accounts for the narration, since the narrator does not adopt a learned position. And finally 'patriarchal' rightly suggests the predominantly male universe of the tale, but patriarchal discourse is a different matter since this would imply a narratorial stance promoting the male characters and values. That this is not the case will appear from my analysis of the use of 'pitee' and related words, and also from the fact that Chaucer's version of the story, unlike Boccaccio's, has women intervene on behalf of the lovers to evoke Theseus' pity after the fight outside the grove (1748–61).

The discourse in *The Knight's Tale* is in fact never consistent enough to deserve such simplified labels as the above. We have seen how some important changes in the poetic design have resulted in a predominantly grave and philosophical tone, but there are many facets of narrative style. Thus the 'high sentence' is not throughout matched by any conventional decorum, as it was claimed by Muscatine[14], but achieved through a complex balance of contrasts in narrative style, expressed in opposing categories as follows:

**seriousness vs. humour**
**high style vs. realism**
**involvement vs. distance**

These contrastive pairs form the backbone of narrative discourse in the tale.[15]

I have here suggested a structuring principle for analysing poetic design and narrative strategy in *The Knight's Tale* to be used as a framework for part of my analysis. In establishing such a framework, I must acknowledge inspiration from especially Salter, who coined the phrase 'the two voices of the poet' to explain what she saw as 'divided purposes' in the narration.[16] Salter did not focus particularly on narrative technique, and 'two voices' in *The Knight's Tale* involves rather too broadly defined categories for my purposes. However, her pioneer study certainly set the agenda for an approach to narration which I offer as the best alternative to the persona-based approaches on the one hand and those approaches on the other hand that does not distinguish complexities of voicing. Paul Oliver has re-marked how relatively few critics are fully aware of 'the constantly chang-ing tones of the narrator's voice' in Chaucer's poetry, and I hasten to add that a recognition of my binary categories alone do not account for the intricate voicing patterns in the tale. So far, however, the oppositions noted above serve as a necessary framework for analysis aiming to explain what Derek Pearsall in another connection has called a 'paradoxical sense of distance and closeness, of alienation and involvement, of apparent objectivity and myopically close focus.'[17]

It must be underlined that my approach stresses Chaucer's narrative voice and technique as a key to interpreting Chaucer and *The Knight's Tale* in particular, but that it does not necessarily contradict other focuses for analysis. I shall end this chapter by considering in turn three related approaches to Chaucerian narrative which are more complementary than contradictory to my line of analysis. All have to do with structuring principles.

The first of these finds its fullest expression in Paul T. Thurston's book *Artistic Ambivalence in Chaucer's Knight's Tale* from 1968. This is a work that assumes a marked persona narration and consequently sees irony and satire almost everywhere, but the method of analysis is worth paying attention to. Building on Muscatine's assessment of symmetries and episodical sequences as overall structuring principles, Thurston analyses basic incongruities and inconsistencies in structure and narration. The essentially New Criticist approach of focusing on conflicts and contrasts pinpoints some remarkable features of composition, perhaps most clearly in Thurston's fine analysis of book I, 1020–34:

> Out of the taas the pilours han hem torn,
> And han hem caried softe unto the tente
> Of Theseus; and he ful soone hem sente
> to Atthenes, to dwellen in prisoun
> Perpetuelly – he nolde no raunsoun.
> And whan this worthy duc hath thus ydon,
> He took his hoost, and hoom he rit anon
> With laurer crowned as a conquerour;
> And ther he lyveth in joye and in honour
> Terme of his lyf; what nedeth wordes mo?
> And in a tour, in angwissh and in wo,
> This Palamon and his felawe Arcite
> For everemoore; ther may no gold hem quite.
> This passeth yeer by yeer and day by day,
> Til it fil ones, in a morwe of May.

Thurston comments:

In these fourteen lines, then, we have the sharpest of contrasts superbly drawn between violence and gentleness, military power and military impotence, the fruits of victory and the bitterness of defeat, and joyous, free action and bitter, enforced inactivity.[18]

He adds that this clash of brief episodes sets the stage for the rest of the narrative, and thus urges us to focus on what I see as Chaucer's brilliantly evoked image of the woeful lovers so to speak squeezed in between Theseus' triumph and Emily's freedom.

Thurston's repeated insistence on humorous or satirical strategies on the part of Chaucer generally weakens his argument. One example is the representation of the love story, on which he concludes:

> Much of the humour and satire in *The Knight's Tale* evolves from the basic inconsistencies between the alleged nature of Arcite's and Palamon's love for Emelye and the actual expression of their love in thoughts, acts, and deeds.[19]

The analysis itself is to the point, because there are indeed basic inconsistencies, as we have seen. Yet the conclusion assumes that the narratorial distance will make us laugh at the lovers' folly, as does Theseus in lines 1791–1810. Surely this at best represents only one side of the coin, since the cruelty of the pagan universe and the tragic outcome of the story add a far more sinister perspective.

The second approach that I offer in extension of my own focus on narratorial voice and technique is V. A. Kolve's already classic study *Chaucer and the Imagery of Narrative* from 1984. Kolve in fact shows little interest in the narrative voice of *The Knight's Tale*, but somewhat vaguely assesses that it is 'grave, mature and dignified' and 'it sounds most like the voice of Theseus, but since even Theseus is sometimes described at a critical distance, we will do better to characterize it simply as sharing a common core of identity.'[20] My modifications to this formulation have already been put forward: the narrative voice cannot be characterized so simply.

However, Kolve has a significant contribution to the issue of narrative structure. Expressing the general assumption that 'medieval narrative calls upon the "inner eye" to a maximum degree' and supporting this with a quotation from Albertus Magnus on the superiority of *metaphorica* to *propria* in a memory system (p 48), he goes on to demonstrate how dominant images serve as a structuring principle in Chaucer's poetry. His analysis of the prison/garden images in *The Knight's Tale* successfully establishes an overall metaphor for what could be regarded as the central conflict of the poem, operating on several levels of its meaning. Whereas Thurston invited us to see the image of the imprisoned lovers versus the free-roaming Emily as setting the stage for the rest of the poem's action, Kolve literally pursues it as the binding element of his analysis. As he records the last prison image in the poem, 'Out of this foule prison of this lyf' (3061, Kolve, p 96), he succeeds in conveying the multiple meanings of the image, which is displayed in variable shades: in the microcosm, especially the physical prison and garden, as well as in the macrocosm, the human prison versus the heavenly garden.

Moreover, Kolve is able to combine the analysis of the prison/garden motif with the philosophical question of human free will implicitly raised in the Boethian passages, thus establishing an overall theme of freedom. That this is related to the theme of order/disorder, which after Muscatine has been regarded as central in most criticism, is suggested by Kolve's analysis of the temple scene in book 3:

> The amphitheater that Theseus builds for the tournament between Palamon and Arcite is to the theme of order in the poem what the prison/garden is to the theme of freedom. It allows Chaucer to assess, in an unusually comprehensive and exploratory way, the possibilities of creating human order within a world apparently governed by chance.[21]

In my own analysis I shall return to the temple scene in order to elaborate on its overall effect. Apart from this brief statement, Kolve largely fails to do so. The focus on art history in this particular analysis points to the strong visual effects, but the temple scene is not placed any further in the overall poetic design.

The third approach to be considered here seems on a surface level to run contrary to Kolve's approach, since it claims that Chaucer's technique is mainly metonymic as opposed to metaphorical. This is argued by Derek Brewer in his article 'Some Metonymic Relationships in Chaucer's Poetry' from 1974. Brewer here makes a case against a modern critical tendency to regard the concept of metaphor as fundamental in poetry, pointing out that Chaucer's poetry works largely in associative patterns. To

support his case he analyses the occurrence of 'sad' and associated adjectives in *The Clerk's Tale* to show how a characteristic chain of meaning
runs through that poem.[22]

If this contradicts Kolve only on a surface level, it is because we are
dealing with basically two ways of approaching elements in the poetic
structure. Kolve establishes central images which become metaphors, for
instance the garden and prison representing conditions in human experience. Equally Griselda's 'sadnesse' could be said to be a central image of
her position in the tale's universe, and on a larger scale a metaphor for the
stoicism associated with her figure. In other words Kolve is mainly concerned with a different level of abstraction in his kind of analysis. And as
Kinney reminds us, 'all literary texts are "metaphoric" in so far as they tend
to proffer an implicit totalizing of significance.'[23]

In connection with her discussion of metaphor and metonymy Kinney
maintains that the distinction is misleading if applied to poetic narrative,
since this form has neither the characteristic paradigmatic or selective
nature of lyric composition, nor the syntagmatic or sequential features of
prose. She concludes with a retort against the theory:

> A poetic narrative is not simply a battleground between the meta-
> phoric and metonymic functions of language. It is rather a text in
> which the energies directed towards structuring content on an ex-
> tended scale and in a unified and significant manner are entangled
> with and perhaps even reconfigured by the local pressures exerted by
> poetic form.[24]

This is a somewhat complicated way of saying that poetic narrative is
neither one or the other; it has a wider complexity of interrelated form and
content. It is not quite fair to Roman Jakobson to dismiss his theory like
this, since he himself never intended it as a general classification of all
literature. Jakobson pointed out some *tendencies* of metaphorical/metony-
mic relations in literature and in fact suggested that as an analytical tool the
distinction might have to be restricted to realistic prose.[25] However, David
Lodge and other practitioners of this kind of analysis have shown that the
theory in an elaborated form is suitable to both prose and lyrical poetry,
including even the mixed forms of modernist literature.[26]

Witnessing Brewer's brief study, there seems to be no good reason why
we should not *also* focus on the metonymic relations in Chaucer's poetry,
as long as we are aware that we cannot in this way classify any of his poems

exhaustively. *The Knight's Tale* was said by Muscatine to follow a 'non-representational, metaphorical method,' and in the sense of being a 'poetic pageant' this is true enough, as also shown in Kolve's analysis.[27] Yet from another angle there are clearly metonymic structures, such as the connected images of animals in the descriptions of Palamon and Arcite.[28] This might tentatively be labelled as a metonymic chain of metaphors.

Concluding the first part of this book we have seen how a number of structuring principles are at work. Thurston, Kolve and Brewer offer alternative frameworks to supplement my own general outline for analysis, frameworks that will be kept in mind as we now turn to the in-depth textual analysis of Chaucer's narrative voice in *The Knight's Tale*.

## Notes to chapter 3

1. In a long tradition of studies in sources and analogues, C. S. Lewis remains a milestone, and it is his title 'What Chaucer really did to *Il Filostrato*' (*Essays and Studies by Members of the English Association*, xvii, 1932) that has chiefly inspired my remark. The term 'shape-shifting' is borrowed from Helen Cooper, 'The Shape-shiftings of the Wife of Bath, 1395–1670' in R. Morse and B. Windeatt, eds., *Chaucer Traditions: Studies in Honour of Derek Brewer* (Cambridge: Cambridge University Press, 1990.)
2. A. C. Spearing, ed., *The Knight's Tale* (Cambridge: Cambridge University Press, 1966), p 2.
3. For diplomatic reasons no names are mentioned here, but see also Derek Pearsall, *The Life of Geoffrey Chaucer* (Oxford: Blackwell, 1992), p 32, who wittily remarks that 'the books he has been credited with a knowledge of by scholars ... would have filled a good-sized monastic library.'
4. Elisabeth Salter, *Chaucer: The Knight's Tale and the Clerk's Tale* (London: Edward Arnold, 1962).
5. David Anderson, *Before The Knight's Tale: Imitation of Classical Epic in Boccaccio's Teseida* (Philadelphia: University of Pennsylvania Press, 1988), chapter 4.
6. F. Anne Payne, *Chaucer and Menippean Satire* (Madison: University of Wisconsin Press, 1981), p 233.
7. Piero Boitani, 'Style, Iconography and Narrative: the Lesson of the *Teseida*' in Boitani, ed., *Chaucer and the Italian Trecento* (Cambridge: Cambridge University Press, 1983), p 191 and p 197. For a scene by scene comparison see the explanatory notes in Benson, ed., *The Riverside Chaucer*.
8. Vittore Branca, ed., *Tutte le Opere di Giovanni Boccaccio* (Maggio: Arnoldo Mandadori, 1964), II, pp 246–7 and Nick Haveley, ed. and transl., *Chaucer's Boccaccio* (Cambridge and Totowa, New Jersey: Boydell & Brewer and Rowman & Littlefield, 1980), p 104. All quotations from the *Teseida* follow these editions.
9. J. A. Burrow, '*The Knight's Tale* and the Ages of Man' in Burrow, ed., *Essays on Medieval Literature* (Oxford: Clarendon Press, 1984), p 47 and Kathleen A. Blake, 'Order and the Noble Life in Chaucer's *Knight's Tale*?' in *Modern Language Quarterly*, 34, 1973, especially 6–7.
10. A. C. Spearing, *Medieval to Renaissance in English Poetry* (Cambridge, Cambridge University Press, 1985), p 49.

11. Clare Regan Kinney, *Strategies of Poetic Narrative: Chaucer, Spenser, Milton, Eliot* (Cambridge: Cambridge University Press, 1992), p 31. Kinney is in fact referring to *Troilus and Criseyde*, but her distinction applies equally well to *The Knight's Tale*.

12. Jennifer Strauss, "'I kan nat seye": The Rhetoric of Narratorial Self-consciousness in Chaucer, Especially in *The Canterbury Tales*' in *AUMLA. Journal of the Australasian Language and Literature Association,* May 1988.

13. Peggy Knapp, *Chaucer and the Social Contest* (New York and London: Routledge, 1990), p 23 and Stephen Knight, *Geoffrey Chaucer* (Oxford: Blackwell, 1986), p 92. The case for the 'archaic' Knight and his tale is argued most persuasively by Bruce C. Cowgill, '*The Knight's Tale* and the 100 Years War' in *Philological Quarterly,* 54, 1975, but Maurice Keen has seriously questioned the foundation for any such assumption about the Knight. See 'Chaucer's Knight, the English Aristocracy and the Crusade' in Scattergood and Sherbourne, eds., *English Court Culture in the Later Middle Ages* (London: Duckworth, 1983).

14. Charles Muscatine, *Chaucer and the French Tradition: A Study in Style and Meaning* (Berkeley and L. A.: University of California Press), pp 173–5. Although he sees *The Knight's Tale* as Chaucer writing at one 'end of the scale' (p 173), leaning on conventional forms, Muscatine shows some awareness of stylistic diversity by stating that 'Chaucer's conventionalism should neither be dismissed nor taken for granted' (p 175).

15. My terminology in this model is based on well established concepts in Chaucer criticism, and consequently no further definitions will be provided. For a stimulating discussion of 'realism' and 'distance' see Morton W. Bloomfield, 'Authenticating Realism and the Realism of Chaucer' in *Thought,* 34, 1964. Also reprinted in Willi Erzgräber, ed., *Geoffrey Chaucer* (Darmstadt: Wissenschaftliche Buchgesellschaft, 1983). Derek Pearsall discusses the 'realism' of *The Knight's Tale* in *The Canterbury Tales* (London: Allen & Unwin, 1985), p 130.

16. Salter, p 23.

17. Paul Oliver, 'Ambiguous Icons: Chaucer's Knight, Parson and Plowman' in Cockson and Loughrey, eds., *Critical Essays on the General Prologue to the Canterbury Tales* (London: Longman, 1989), p 82 and Derek Pearsall 1992, pp 197–8.

18. Paul T. Thurston, *Artistic Ambivalence in Chaucer's Knight's Tale* (Gainesville: University of Florida Press, 1968), pp 78–9.

19. Thurston, pp 227–8.

20. V. A. Kolve, *Chaucer and the Imagery of Narrative* (London: Edward Arnold, 1984), p 134.

21. Kolve, p 105.

22. Derek Brewer, 'Some Metonymic Relationships in Chaucer's Poetry' in Brewer, *Chaucer: The Poet as Storyteller* (Houndsmill and London: MacMillan, 1984).

23. Kinney, p 9.

24. Kinney, p 9.

25. The relevant articles are Roman Jakobson, 'Two Aspects of Language and Two Types of Aphasic Disturbances,' in Jakobson, *Selected Writings, vol. II* (The Hague and Paris: Mouton, 1971) and 'Closing Statement: Linguistics and Poetics' in Thomas A. Sebeok, ed., *Style in Language* (New York and London: Technology Press of Massachusetts Institute of Technology and John Wiley & Sons, 1960).

26. See David Lodge, 'The Language of Modernist Fiction: Metaphor and Metonymy' in Bradbury and McFarlane, eds., *Modernism 1890–1930* (Harmondsworth: Penguin, 1976) and Lodge, *The Modes of Modern Writing* (London: Edward Arnold, 1977).

27. Charles Muscatine, 'Form, Texture and Meaning in Chaucer's *Knight's Tale*' in Wagenknecht ed., *Chaucer: Modern Essays in Criticism* (New York: Oxford University Press, 1959), p 69.

28. Among many critical observations on this point, the most exhaustive treatment remains Jeffrey Heltermann, 'The Dehumanizing Metamorphoses of the *Knight's Tale*' in *English Literary History,* 38, 1971.

# Part II

CHAPTER 4

# Narratorial Self-consciousness

We have established in the previous chapters that the Knight from *The General Prologue* is only present as a character in the initial frame of the tale and in its very last line. In the analysis I shall consequently refer to 'the Knight' in this part of the poem only, whereas 'the narrator' is used elsewhere, bearing in mind the reservations about this simplified term that were expressed in the first part.

When the storytelling game gets under way and the lot falls to the Knight, he wastes no time in starting his tale. The introduction to the subject matter up to the triumphant entry of Theseus into Athens occupies only 26 lines as opposed to two books in the *Teseida*, and indeed it contains a very concise summary of Theseus' warfare. Part of the account is given when the Knight has in fact broken off his storyline in order to explain that he has not got the time to render the details of Theseus' exploits:

> And certes, if it nere to long to heere,
> I wolde have toold yow fully the manere
> How wonnen was the regne of Femenye
> ...
> But al that thyng I moot as now forbere.
> I have, God woot, a large feeld to ere,
> And wayke been the oxen in my plough.
> The remenant of the tale is long ynough.
> I wol nat letten eek noon of this route;
> Lat every felawe telle his tale aboute,
> And lat se now who shal the soper wynne;
> And ther I lefte, I wol ageyn bigynne.
> (875–7 & 885–92)

This is the first of a long line of *occupatios* in the tale, serving the double purpose of excusing narratorial editing, especially abbreviation, and of still being able to render the essentials of the subject matter that must otherwise be left out. As part of the narrative strategy this is a favourite Chaucerian device in the struggle for a 'goal-determined narrative design' (as discussed in chapter 3), but it is also highly conventional in medieval literature as one of many ways of drawing attention to the storytelling itself. I myself will now take a dilation in my analysis of this passage, because I want to consider briefly that convention and Chaucer's use of it in general.

In the popular medieval romances, which draw heavily upon an oral tradition, we can be almost sure to find a kind of poetic contract set up at the beginning of the story, asking the audience to listen and pay attention in return for the poetic efforts of the composer. A few examples will suffice:

> Whoso wyll a stounde dwelle
> Of mykyll myrght Y may you telle
> ...
> Of a lady fayr and fre
> Her name was called Emaré,
> (*Emaré*, 19–20 & 22–3)

> Lytyll and mykyll, olde and yonge,
> Listenyth now to my talkynge,
> Of whome Y wyll yow [k]ythe;
> (*Octavian*, 1–3)

> Jesu Chryst, that barne blythe,
> Gyff hom joy that lovus to lythe
> Of ferlys that befell.
> A la[y] of Breyten long Y soght
> And owt thereof a tale have y broght,
> That lufly is to tell.
> (*Sir Gowther*, 25–30)[1]

Here we have part of the tradition associated with formulaic compositional technique, but it may of course well have had a very real background, since storytellers in an oral tradition will have had to ask for silence and draw attention to themselves. The narratorial self-consciousness can in some cases result in a voice that is beyond the merely conventional, as in the naively enthusiastic 'That lufly is to tell' from *Sir Gowther*, but romance narrators usually draw more attention to their sources than to themselves.

Yet by and large they tell their stories in straightforward, uninterrupted chronological sequence. For instance the narrator in *Octavian* uses the linefillers 'Yn bokys of ryme hyt is tolde,' 'In romans as we rede,' and 'These clerkys seyn soo' in each of the first three stanzas to (conventionally) indicate the authorities behind the story; but then he turns the focus fully on the dramatic story, which is rendered without a narrative break for the rest of its 1800 lines, allowing only a brief concluding prayer. There are only two or three short remarks indicating the narrator's presence, notably 'I wyll you telle forwhy./ Grete dele hyt ys to telle' (204–5).

In connection with a discussion of Chaucer's early poetry Derek Pearsall writes:

> Already, too, the characteristic Chaucerian 'voice' is to be heard, not strikingly dissimilar from the voice of the unsophisticated narrator in the English romances..:

Pearsall is referring to what he calls 'a conversational and gossipy tone, the liveliness, the tags, the syntactical padding of familiar address,'[2] and insofar I agree to the parallel. However, I hope to demonstrate that the Chaucerian voice is strikingly different exactly because of a very sophisticated administration of narratorial self-consciousness. Let alone the obvious difference in narrative control and technique.

In some of Chaucer's early poetry we find the delicately sensitive, often self-ironically simplistic narrator whose presence lends no comparison with either the truly naive English romance narrators, nor the conventional young dreamer-narrator in the *The Romance of the Rose*. First, an example from *The Book of the Duchess*:

> Whan I had red thys tale wel
> And overloked hyt everydel,
> Me thoghte wonder yf hit were so,
> For I had never herd speke or tho
> Of noo goddes that koude make
> Men to slepe, ne for to wake,
> For I ne knew never god but oon.
> (231–7)

Besides including a delightful fictional lie – Chaucer's poetry is of course full of knowledge about other gods, Morpheus included – this piece expresses consciousness about the nature of the fiction and the role of the poet-narrator by playfully guiding the audience through a pagan world with realistic common sense.

In *The House of Fame* the dreamer-narrator is directly addressed as 'Geffrey' (729), and we get some very self-conscious insight into this fictively author-identified narrator, eg in the much celebrated passage in which Chaucer lets himself be mockingly represented as a dry bookworm by the eagle:

> For when thy labour doon al ys,
> And hast mad alle thy rekenynges,
> In stede of reste and newe thynges
> Thou goost hom to thy hous anoon,
> And, also domb as any stoon,
> Thou sittest at another book
> Tyl fully daswed ys thy look;
> And lyvest thus as an heremyte,
> Although thyn abstynence ys lyte.
> (*The House of Fame*, 652–60)

This is on the verge of breaking the fiction, because of the probably realistic self-irony of the real Chaucer, portrayed as being prone to solitary occupation with books, maybe in the good company of wine, as the last line indicates.[3] *The House of Fame* as a whole presents a lively picture of this fictional counterpart to Chaucer and displays a self-consciousness of such prominence that the narrator may be viewed as the main character.

The unique Chaucerian voice is found in a parallel scene at the end of *The Parliament of Fowls*:

> I wook, and othere bokes tok me to,
> To reede upon, and yit I rede alwey.
> I hope, ywis, to rede so som day
> That I shal mete som thyng for to fare
> The bet, and thus to rede I nyl nat spare.
> (695–9)

The humorous self-characterization is matched by a sincere zest for poetic exploration ('to fare the bet'), if not for personal achievement on a general scale. The first line of the poem is 'The lyf so short, the craft so long to lerne,' and although this refers specifically to 'love,' we realize that the act of poetic creation is also very much on the agenda.

Finally in this dilation let us turn to *The Legend of Good Women*, which was also among the works considered in my introductory discussion of authorial presence in chapter 1. Here I demonstrated how a poetic contract is established in all of Chaucer's major works, explicating the poetic scope and intention, we may now add with a superior clarity and self-consciousness in comparison with the popular literature, indeed nearly all literature of his day. In the F version of the *Legend*, presumably composed shortly after *Troilus & Criseyde* and the first version of *The Knight's Tale*, Chaucer has developed an even keener self-consciousness as a poet than in the early poems. He now ventures to display his poetic achievements, characteristically in connection with a long, self-directed slander-campaign, the result of a heated discussion between the God of Love and his queen which starts off by diminishing Chaucer the poet to a status lower than a worm (F 315–430). The indirect poetic upgrading of himself comes in queen Alceste's slighting defence of his work:

> Al be hit that he kan nat wel endite,
> Yet hath he maked lewed folk delyte
> To serve yow, in preysinge of your name.
> He made the book that hight the Hous of Fame,
> and eke the Deeth of Blaunche the Duchesse,
> And the Parlement of Foules, as I gesse,
> And al the love of Palamon and Arcite
> of Thebes, thogh the storye ys knowen lyte;
> And many an ympne for your halydayes,
> That highten balades, roundels, virelayes;
> And for to speke of other holynesse,
> He hath in prose translated Boece,
> And made the lyf also of Seint Cecile.
> He made also, goon ys a gret while,
> Origenes upon the Maudeleyne.
> Hym oughte now to have the lesse peyne;
> He hath maad many a lay and many a thing.
> (*The Legend of Good Women*, F 414–30)

The display of the canon of his works, repeated with revisions in the G version and in the *Retraction* to *The Canterbury Tales*, shows Chaucer's ultimate self-consciousness as a great poet, yet humbly mixed with self-effacement.

The self-consciousness appears the stronger when Chaucer gets to exhibit his capacity to create different narrative voices in the *Tales;* as I have stressed earlier not necessarily through the pilgrim *personae*, but to a higher extent through the multiplicity of genres. In *The Knight's Tale* as in the *Legend* there are some obvious reasons for narratorial involvement of the *occupatio*-kind, since both works involve significant reductions of material. But the self-consciousness connected with the handling of genre and story goes far beyond that. Let us now return to the opening of *The Knight's Tale* to consider the nature of the self-conscious display here.

In the *occupatio* in lines 875–92 there is an obvious revision of the 'Palamon and Arcite' mentioned in the extract from the *Legend*: The Knight refers specifically to the storytelling game and addresses the narratees, the other pilgrims. We saw in chapter 2 how this framework is only evoked once more, in the very last line of the poem: 'And God save al this faire compaignye! Amen.' It seems as if Chaucer has wanted to affix the tale to the Knight only because the genre fits him well – it is after all a tale about chivalry – not because any further integration is intended. However, the fact that it is the Knight and not for instance the Miller is important, as a comparison with *The Miller's Tale* will show. J. A. Burrow is among the many critics who have pointed to *The Miller's Tale* as an exact parallel to *The Knight's Tale* in its general outline, the main difference being only that it consistently operates on a different social level.[4]

The narratorial self-consciousness in *The Knight's Tale* has to do with the social level of its discourse, but this has to do with Chaucer the poet as much as with the Knight. The elegant metaphor in lines 886–7 implicitly suggests the relatively high social status of the narrator, ie of someone who is bothered about the effects of possible delays and who nobly understates his capacity ('wayke been the oxen in my plough'). It is tempting to compare with the narrator of the popular romance *Sir Isumbras*, whose social code is markedly different. This is seen at the beginning of the poem when he admires his hero:

I wyll you tell of a knyghte
...
A man he was ryche ynowghe
Of oxen to drawe in his plowghe,
(*Sir Isumbras,* 7 and 13–4)

Although a verbal echo, the contrast is striking, first of all because the discourse in *The Knight's Tale* generally matches the social code of its subject matter. In other words, the narrator is capable of verbal decorum and very openly conscious of this fact.[5]

The *occupatios* and their rhetorical variants of *diminutio* and *abbrevatio* continue throughout the tale. There are numerous brief excuses for narrative summary, eg 'But shortly for to speken of this thyng' (985), 'But shortly for to tellen is myn entente' (1000), and 'But of that storie list me nat to write' (1201), and here it is difficult not to imagine the poet rather than the narrator at work, cutting down on Boccaccio's long story, especially since the act of writing is referred to.

A more complicated narrative technique is displayed in some of the longer *occupatios*. A. C. Spearing cites lines 2197–2206, the description of the feast given by Theseus, as an example of Chaucer's virtuosity in weaving a comprehensive description into a tight form, and indeed this is a delightful aside from the narrator.[6] Yet again he refuses to let himself be carried away:

Of al this make I now no mencioun.
But al th'effect; that thynketh me the beste.
Now cometh the point, and herkneth if yow leste.
(2206–8)

So, we are led to believe, 'th'effect' is the main concern. The expression 'th'effect' crops up also in lines 1189 and 1487, indicating the narratorial impatience to get on with the story.

When we reach the longest *occupatio* in the tale, which comes near the end (2919–66), it becomes difficult to accept the sincerity of the narrator's impatience. Here we find an extremely elaborate and complicated description of Arcite's funeral ceremony in a paratactic sentence form, bound together by no less than sixteen 'ne'-constructions. These serve to inform us about what the narrator is *not* going to tell us, allowing him at the same time to do exactly this. Thus in lines 2919–24 the narrator says:

But how the fyr was maked upon highte,
Ne eek the names that the trees highte,
As ook, firre, birch, aspe, alder, holm, popler,
Wylugh, elm, plane, assh, box, chasteyn, lynde, laurer,
Mapul, thorn, bech, hasel, ew, whippeltree –

How they weren feld shal nat be toold for me;

It is difficult to think of names of trees he has left out in this almost absurdly long list. This is a purely ornamental piece of description that slows down the narrative pace considerably, and no doubt a passage which will have been more pleasing for the medieval than for the modern audience.

The circumstancial descriptive passages, on the other hand, are a matter of self-conscious narratorial concern elsewhere in the poem. Maybe most conspicuously at the beginning of book III:

I trowe men wolde deme it negligence
If I foryete to tellen the dispense
Of Theseus, that gooth so bisily
To maken up the lystes roially,
(1881–4)

Clearly the narratorial claim is here that a certain decorum, including celebrations of pomp and circumstance, is to be expected as part of the hidden contract of storytelling. Needless to say this is fully in line with medieval handbooks of rhetoric, and so we see Chaucer writing very much according to this tradition here. Still the descriptive passages which fill up most of book III are also among the artistically most innovative in poetic style, a point to be considered further in chapter 6.

The pace of narration *is* slow compared to *The Miller's Tale* and the other fabliaux, but this is justified by the high style and 'sentence.' Compared to popular romances *The Knight's Tale* rarely indulges in description without any seeming purpose, and it might in fact be argued that the slow movement is both deliberate and an integrated part of the poem's meaning. Certainly the long philosophical dilations add to this impression. Paul Strohm supports this view in a fine analysis of time and narrative form, showing how the static quality of the narration is achieved partly through the slow progress of each episode, and partly through a series of time markers that work against 'eventful temporality,' such as 'perpetuelly' (1024), 'yeer by yeer and day by day' (1033) and 'By processe and by lengthe of certeyn yeres' (2967). Strohm appropriately refers also to Muscatine's analysis which so significantly established the principles of composition, summed up in the expression 'poetic pageant.'[7]

In connection with his discussion of narrative pace, Strohm raises the question of genre, preferring the simpler 'storie' to both romance and epic, although allowing for elements of both of these.[8] I would agree that this is the best solution, cf also Chaucer's general designation in *The Miller's Prologue*, 'Of storial thyng that toucheth gentilesse,' (3179) which follows shortly after *The Knight's Tale* has been described by the other pilgrims as 'a noble storie/ and worthy for to drawen to memorie.' (3111–2) As we saw in the quotation from *The Legend of Good Women* (F 414–30, above), Chaucer was extremely conscious about genre forms, but having blended romance and epic with philosophical passages and the strong narratorial presence to such a great extent, it is no surprise that he lets his pilgrims choose the simpler, general classification. What is important is the addition, a *noble* story, signifying the generic code. In this way 'the genre shapes (but does not determine) the work,' as Ridley has it (cf chapter 1, p 23). Accordingly, the narrative pace is subject to generic demands, but Chaucer manipulates with audience expectations by constantly having his narrator draw attention to it.

The narratorial struggle to convince the audience that every effort is being made to proceed with the story is only partly successful, but this is certainly deliberate, as Chaucer's real effort is aimed at being able to dwell on the storial matter rather than the story itself. There is some playful irony in the fact that the narrator's efforts often work contrary to his declared intentions, but such poetic licence provides artistic elegance and probably goodwill as well as admiration from a medieval audience. For a modern audience this may in some cases not be so, especially if the irony is seen as reflecting the narrator's incompetence or self-justification. An example of this is Lee Patterson's persona-based interpretation in which one conclusion is that

> The *Knight's Tale* shows us the chivalric mind engaged in an act of self-legitimization that simultaneously and secretly undoes itself.[9]

Such a view cannot be valid since the 'self-legitimization' of the narratorial interventions is used in more or less the same way everywhere in Chaucer's poetry, as we have seen. Especially the *occupatio* is a conventionalized rhetorical device whose apparently self-contradictory nature must not be taken literally, and Chaucer is merely a particularly elegant practitioner, fully aware of its range of possibilities.

The extensive use of *occupatio* and the many other examples of narratorial self-consciousness in *The Knight's Tale* can also be regarded as yet another structuring device. Charles Moseley has a comment on this point:

> The individual narrative blocks, framed by the narratorial voice, are built into the larger units of the four separate books.[10]

This is in line with the idea of an essentially episodical structure, and it is correctly observed that the narrator frames the episodes through his interruptions. In some cases this is done merely by a quick transitional remark:

> This is th'effect and his entente pleyn.
> Now wol I turne to Arcite ageyn,
> (1487–8)

> And in this wise I lette hem fightyng dwelle,
> And forth I wole of Theseus yow telle.
> (1661–2)

> But stynte I wole of Theseus a lite,
> And speke of Palamon and of Arcite.
> (2093–4)

These are formulaic and conventional transitions, but as we have seen, especially the *occupatio*-interruptions tend to be more elaborate, and in the case of the *occupatio* describing the funeral rites after Arcite's death we have in fact a full narrative block disguised as a transitional interruption.

As it will be seen, the narratorial self-consciousness has multiple functions in the tale, yet primary among these is the highlighting of composition and the role of the poet. As V. A. Kolve remarks:

> *The Knight's Tale* is the most insistently "artificial" of all Chaucer's major poems, constantly calling attention to itself as a thing "made."[11]

'Artificial' apparently both in the sense of 'a thing made' and in the sense of a piece of art. In this chapter we have seen the poetic voice in its most conspicuous shape, assuming a lively, character-like presence. As a side-effect we get a glimpse of 'the poet at work', being conscious of his art in struggling with control over some very complex material.

## Notes to chapter 4

1. All three romances and *Sir Isumbras*, cited below, are reprinted in Maldwyn Mills, ed., *Six Middle English Romances* (London: Dent Everyman's Library, 1973). The references are to this edition. My brief discussion of composition in romances refers generally to the Parry/Lord theory of oral composition and to the applications of this to the Middle English Romances.

2. Derek Pearsall, *The Life of Geoffrey Chaucer* (Oxford: Blackwell, 1992), p 72.

3. This would fit well with our knowledge of Chaucer's allowance of a daily pitcher of wine from 1374–78. See Derek Pearsall, p 95.

4. For this comparison and for an excellent assessment of the influence of genres on *The Canterbury Tales* see J. A. Burrow, *Medieval Writers and Their Work: Middle English Literature and its Background 1100–1500* (Oxford: Oxford University Press, 1982), pp 77–85.

5. This corresponds with the findings of Jennifer Strauss in her analysis of narratorial self-consciousness in *The Canterbury Tales* generally. Strauss distinguishes three audience-directed concerns, first the management of style, secondly the verbal decorum of the tale, and thirdly the management of its available space. See '"I kan nat seye": The Rhetoric of Narratorial Self-consciousness in Chaucer, Especially in *The Canterbury Tales*' in *AUMLA. Journal of the Australasian Language and Literature Association*, May 1988, especially 166.

6. A. C. Spearing, ed., *The Knight's Tale* (Cambridge: Cambridge University Press, 1966), pp 35–6.

7. Paul Strohm, *Social Chaucer* (Cambridge: Harvard University Press, 1989). The examples are Strohm's, cited from p 131. I have referred to Muscatine's analysis in more detail on pp 11–13.

8. Strohm, p 130. Besides Anderson, discussed in chapter 3, other critics have applied the label *epic*, for example Paul A. Olson, *The Canterbury Tales and the Good Society* (Princeton: Princeton University Press, 1986), pp 61–2 and John Finlayson, '*The Knight's Tale*: The Dialogue of Romance, Epic, and Philosophy' in *The Chaucer Review*, 27, 1992. Problems with applying strict genre conventions to Chaucer and to *The Knight's Tale* in particular are discussed in Susan Crane, 'Medieval Romance and Feminine Difference in *The Knight's Tale*' in *Studies in the Age of Chaucer*, 12, 1990. Cf. also Burrow, note 4.

9. Lee Patterson, *Chaucer and the Subject of History* (London: Routledge, 1991), p 169. For a fuller account of Patterson's view of narration turn to my chapter 2, pp 32–4.

10. Charles Moseley, ed., *Geoffrey Chaucer: The Knight's Tale* (Harmondsworth: Penguin, 1987), p 55.

11. V. A. Kolve, *Chaucer and the Imagery of Narrative* (London: Edward Arnold, 1984), p 135.

# CHAPTER 5

# Humour, Realism, and Distance

Dichotomies such as those set up in the model on page 50 establish general contrasts and oppositions in narrative style, delicately balanced by Chaucer, but the scale is tipped in the direction of the grave and philosophical tone that characterizes the poem as a whole. The principle of contrasting styles is a mark of distinction in Chaucer's poetic mastery, and in *The Knight's Tale* some extremely subtle effects are achieved. In this chapter we shall see how humour, realism and distance are employed in the narration to enforce an impression of narrative control and to throw the contrasting elements of seriousness, high style and involvement into relief.

Part of the analysis has been carried out already in the discussions of narratorial self-consciousness and narrative strategy: Distance and detachment occur frequently, especially in the representation of the love story, and in such examples as the *demande d'amour* at the end of book I ('Yow loveres axe I now this questioun...') and the disclaimer in book II, 1459–60 ('Who koude ryme in Englyssh proprely/ His martirdom?') the tone is wonderfully light and carefree. If we now take a step further and consider these examples in their exact context, we will see the refinement of the technique. The *demande d'amour* follows two parallel complaints from Arcite and Palamon, both marked by a heavy, philosophical tone, for instance 1251–2 and 1303–4:

Allas, why pleynen folk so in commune
On purveiaunce of God, or of Fortune

Thanne seyde he, "O crueel goddes that governe
This world with byndyng of youre word eterne,"

Lamenting exclamations such as 'allas' and apostrophes such as 'O' are characteristic of the high style of these passages (see further the analysis in chapter 7), and it is as if Chaucer deliberately wants to destroy the credibility of this high rhetoric from the lovers by juxtaposing it so sharply with the narratorial playfulness.

In the second example, 1459–60, this tendency to be down-to-earth and not let the tale be too high-flown and serious is even more outspoken. The narratorial comment follows an account of Palamon's sufferings, characterized by a tight clustering of words denoting his misery, and underlined poetically by long, heavy vowel sounds:

> In derknesse and horrible and strong prisoun
> Thise seven yeer hath seten Palamoun
> Forpyned, what for wo and for distresse
> Who feeleth double soor and hevynesse
> But Palamon, ...
> (1451–5)

The swiftness and lightness of the poetry following these lines enforces the humorous distancing effect:

> Who koude ryme in Englyssh proprely
> His martirdom? For sothe it am nat I;
> Therefore I passe as lightly as I may.
> (1459–61)

Parallel to this is the narrator's comment 'What sholde I al day of his wo endite?' (1380), following the slightly ridiculous behaviour of Arcite in courtly love. Chaucer must have enjoyed exaggerating the courtly code in this delicately detailed portrait of the lover's pains. At least he has extended the description here in comparison with Boccaccio's, adding considerably more swooning and wailing, besides twisting some of the images to allow for a touch of everyday realism to interfere with the all too artificial nature of courtly love. Notice the familiarization of the italicized half-lines below:

> And if he herde song or instrument
> Thanne wolde he wepe, *he myghte nat be stent.*
> So feble eek were his spiritz, and so lowe,
> And chaunged so, that no man koude knowe
> His speche nor his voys, *though men it herde.*
> (1367–71, my italics)

It is as if Chaucer on the one hand is fascinated by the convention of courtly love – as also indicated by his use of the tradition in most of his love poems – and on the other hand enjoys a realistic detachment from its stereotyped patterns. His audience are allowed to stop and think about the fact that Palamon and Arcite are young and foolish lovers. In book I and the first half of book II especially, when they are as yet uneducated by the tragic events of their later experiences, the lovers are continually pinned down by the narrator's gentle, but also comic realistic filter. A final example from this part is from just before the fight outside the grove. Here we meet Arcite in the shape of Philostrate, seemingly released from his earlier melancholy. Yet his temporary happiness is quickly lost, and this is commented on with a striking comparison:

> Whan that Arcite hadde romed al his fille,
> And songen al the roundel lustily,
> Into a studie he fil sodeynly,
> As doon thise loveres in hir queynte geres,
> Now in the crope, now doun in the breres,
> Now up, now doun, as boket in a welle.
> (1528–33)

In discussing this passage, Barbara Nolan has characterized the narratorial attitude well, even though she attributes the gentle irony to a Knight-persona (see also my chapter 2):

> With his homely metaphors and his easy generalizations ... he offers us a mature, comic, and commonsensical view of Arcite's experience which the young lover cannot possibly share.[1]

Both Arcite and Palamon are in fact treated with a disrespect close to ridicule in the scenes analysed here, and in the fight outside the grove their behaviour reaches a low point. Arcite defies the bond of sworn brotherhood and even challenges its existence altogether (1604–5), whereas Palamon on his part ignobly passes sentence on Arcite and not just himself when they have been discovered by Theseus (1714–41). With these changes to Boccaccio's story Chaucer must have wanted to stress the all too human reality behind the chivalrous and courtly codes of these 'two noble kinsmen'. What we witness in the fight is the animal passions of men, poetically reinforced by similes comparing the two knights to tigers, lions and boars.[2]

The intervention of Theseus to stop the fight, and the intervention of the queen and her company of ladies to spare their lives mark the turning point for Palamon and Arcite, but first Theseus takes over from the narrator as commentator in a passage which serves as comic relief after the dramatic tension:

Lo heere this Arcite and this Palamoun,

...

Now looketh, is nat that an heigh folye?
Who may been a fool but if he love?
Bihoold, for Goddes sake that sit above,
Se how they blede! Be they noght wel arrayed?

...

But this is yet the beste game of alle,
That she for whom they han this jolitee
Kan hem therfore as muche thank as me.
She woot namoore of al this hoote fare,
By God, than woot a cokkow or an hare!
(1791, 1798–1801, 1806–10)

The irony of the situation – fighting over a lady who is completely unaware that she is loved and idolized by the two knights – is spelled out here, and moreover the language is sharpened compared to the narratorial comments. There is the distancing effect of '*this* Arcite' and '*this* Palamon', which perhaps because of its more widespread use in Middle English should not be taken too seriously, but 'heigh folye', 'beste game', 'this jolitee' and especially 'hoote fare' are semi-vulgar expressions of contempt for the foolishness of the lovers. 'Se how they blede' is moreover a rather cynical joke on their expense, although Theseus restores some sympathy by excusing youthful folly, as he himself has been in their situation: 'For in my tyme a servant was I oon.' (1814)

Elisabeth Salter has stressed the paradoxical sense of relief that this rather crude passage gives rise to:

The robust, even coarse, common-sense of Theseus provides com-
fortable reading; like the good-temper of the 'narrator', it offsets the

unpleasantness of much that has already happened, and much that is likely to happen.[3]

Implicit in this precise statement is a notion of the far from merry note struck in the representation of the theme of love so far and of the worse that is to follow. In assessing the importance of comedy and ironic distance we must not underestimate the background on which these elements operate.

The temporary comfort afforded by Theseus' decree at the end of book II is largely undermined in book III (cf also chapter 6). In the representation of Theseus' amphitheatre and the prayers of Palamon, Emily and Arcite the tone of the poem changes to a far more sinister note, and the humorous comments disappear. Scrupulous critics have been able to trace one or two possibly funny narratorial remarks, such as the mention of the price of the paint (2087–8) and the narrator's wink in the eye as he 'dar nat telle' how Emily went about taking her bath (2282–6),[4] but by and large there is very little relief from the high seriousness of the descriptions. Only when the now highly involved narrator bubbles over with enthusiasm a few times does the tone become lighter, eg:

> To fighte for a lady, benidicitee!
> It were a lusty sighte for to see.
> (2115–16)

However, as the scene with the gods at the end of book III admonishes, the outcome of the story is not going to be so pleasant as indicated in this remark. Book IV, as a contrast, starts with a scene that might make the audience forget the uncomfortable and disturbing tone of book III. This is the lively preparation for the great tournament, focusing on the display of chivalry and the streets swarming with people:

> The sheeldes brighte, testeres, and trappures
> Gold-hewen helmes, hauberkes, cote-armures;
> Lordes in parementz on hir courseres,
> Knyghtes of retenue, and eek squires
> ...
> The paleys ful of peple up and doun,
> Heere thre, ther ten, holdynge hir questioun,

Dyvynynge of thise Theban knyghtes two.
Somme seyden thus, some seyde "it shal be so";
Somme helden with hym with the blake berd,
Somme with the balled, somme with the thikke herd;
Somme seyde he looked grymme, and he wolde fighte:
(2499–2502 and 2513–19)

The sheer forcefulness of the poetry with its light movement, the alliter-
ations ('testeres', 'trappures' and 'Gold-hewen helmes, hauberkes') and the
anaphora in lines 2516–19 helps create a brilliant sound-picture, and this is
reinforced by the impressionistic and colourful narration. The idiom is
partly chivalric, partly popular in an ingenious mixture, and the scene
seems also realistically recreated. For instance the discussions among the
people about the outcome of the tournament would be easily recognized
by a modern audience with any enthusiasm for great sporting events. This
is an archetypal situation before a special public occasion, and of course
Chaucer will have had expert knowledge of this particular kind of public
entertainment from his own participation in arranging tournaments at
Smithfield. The narratorial enthusiasm apparent in this scene could well
reflect Chaucer's own stance.

This is not to say that the dangerous aspect of the tournament is
suppressed. The fact that Theseus decrees a ban of certain weapons and
speaks against mortal battle reminds the audience of the potential dark side
of battle and jousting. The tone by contrast becomes serene and pompous
as Theseus' official decree is juxtaposed to the chatter of the common
people, and a distancing effect is achieved quite literally when Theseus is
shown 'at a wyndow set,/ Arrayed right as he were a god in trone.'
(2528–9) The pomp and circumstance from now on continues through to
the tournament scene itself, and the narrative style becomes reportage in a
high style that echoes the emblematic presentation of the lists for the
tournament in book III. Alliteration again adds to a forceful poetic representation of a magnificent display:

Out brest the blood with stierne stremes rede;
With myghty maces the bones they tobreste.
He thurgh the thikkeste of the throng gan threste;
Ther stomblen steedes stronge, and doun gooth al,
He rolleth under foot as dooth a bal;

(2610–14)

The last line in this quotation provides a humorous simile that almost breaks the illusion of splendour, since knights perhaps ought not to roll in the fashion of a ball. This is once more a small homely detail showing Chaucer's zest for playfulness and adding a realistic narratorial touch to the fantastic scenery.

At the initial joyful outcome of the tournament, Chaucer's source states that Emilia takes an active part in acknowledging Arcita's victory, and she is given a long speech of praise by Boccaccio, part of which I have quoted in chapter 3, pp 41. About Chaucer's Emily it says only:

> And she agayn hym caste a freendlich ye
> (For wommen for to speken in comune,
> Thei folwen alle the favour of Fortune)
> And was al his chiere, as in his herte.
> (2680–3)

Some critics have frowned at this antifeminist comment and thus pointed to a good reason why lines 2681–2 have been left out in some manuscripts, but the joke is quite brilliant if taken as a gentle parody of Boccaccio's type of heroine, and we have seen elsewhere how Chaucer likes to distance himself from the stereotyped poetry of courtly romance. If the joke is misplaced at all, it is only because of the serious context of the following scene with Arcite's accident, but it could also be maintained that it enforces the contrast of the sudden movement from 'wele to wo'.

It may well be examples like the small jokes we have been considering that made a stern Victorian poet and critic like Matthew Arnold dislike Chaucer for his lack of high seriousness, as suggested by Michael Alexander.[5] Even the death of Arcite fails to follow the patterns of a heroic death: Arcite dies not in battle but after accidentally falling from his horse, and the realism in the description of the accident spoils any vision of grandeur. It says simply:

> His brest tobrosten with his sadel-bowe
> As blak he lay as any cole or crowe,
> So was the blood yronnen in his face
> Anon he was yborn out of the place,
> (2691–4)

The simile 'as any cole or crowe' seems especially anti-heroic, and the rashness with which Arcite is carried off defies any glorification. It may be argued that Arcite is not dead yet in this scene, but the death scene itself supports the initial impression. In the light of the extensive critical attention to this scene, and because of its obvious importance in the poem, it will be worthwhile to consider it at some length.

After a dilation in which some hope is nourished for Arcite's recovery, and in which suspense about this possibility is blended with forced cheerfulness because of Theseus' decree 'To stynten alle rancour and envye,' (2732) the actual death of Arcite comes as a shocking contrast. We have once again been led to believe that all is well, since after three days of 'feeste' the knights of the tournament all leave Theseus' court, and 'Ther was namoore but "Fare wel, have good day!"' (2740) We learn after a brief transitional remark from the narrator how deceptive this assurance is:

Of this bataille I wol namoore endite,
But speke of Palamon and of Arcite.
Swelleth the brest of Arcite, and the soore
Encresseth at his herte moore and moore,
The clothered blood, for any lechecraft,
Corrupteth, and is in his bouk ylaft,
That neither veyne-blood, ne ventusynge,
Ne drynke of herbes may ben his helpynge.
The vertu expulsif, or animal,
Fro thilke vertu cleped natural
Ne may the venym voyden ne expelle.
The pipes of his longes gonne to swelle,
And every lacerte in his brest adoun
Is shent with venym and corrupcioun.
Hym gayneth neither, for to gete his lif,
Vomyt upward, ne dounward laxatif.
Al is tobrosten thilke regioun;
Nature hath now no dominacioun.
And certeinly, ther Nature wol nat wirche,
Fare wel phisik! Go ber the man to chirche!
This al and som, that Arcita moot dye;
(2741–61)

This passage is not just a piece of realism, it is an exposition of medieval

anatomy and thus written in a different code of language from the rest of
the tale: versified science, so to speak.[6] It is remarkable that Chaucer
should have chosen such a longwinded and minute description of the
collapse of the bodily functions to replace the heroic passing of Boccaccio's
Arcita. If the idea is simply to regret that once dead is dead for good, as
indicated in lines 2759–60, then there is no reason why Chaucer should
not have been satisfied with something on the lines of the following brief
remark from *Troilus and Criseyde*, book V, 741–2:

> But al to late comth the letuarie
> Whan men the cors unto the grave carie.

Instead we are spared absolutely nothing of what must surely also to the
medieval mind have seemed the most revolting and repulsive medical
details about the process of death. There must have been a good reason for
this almost all too conspicuous narrative strategy.

Among a wide range of critical opinions the most extreme, yet perhaps
also the simplest explanation is offered by Derek Pearsall. Discussing the
'instability of tone' in this and other passages of the tale, Pearsall airs the
idea that in trying to 'modulate the poem ... from its predominantly minor
key ... Chaucer has not yet mastered the delicate techniques of narrative
control.'[7] The anti-glorification of Chaucer in this brave statement almost
matches that of Arcite's death in the passage under scrutiny. That it is a
flaw in narration is, however, a less far-fetched bid than some other critical
contributions (also discussed by Pearsall), for example that the passage
reflects the Knight's incompetence as narrator or is indicative of a general
parody of romance and chivalry. I have already refuted such views in
chapter 2.

If we accept that the description is a slightly exaggerated attempt to
provide an antidote to the high seriousness of the immediate poetic
context, it will also be possible to answer some of the justified outcries
from critics who have been upset by it, for instance Kathleen A. Blake:

> Such a death cannot be read as poetic justice. It is too disproportion-
> ally awful for Arcite to deserve.[8]

Blake herself uses the description as part of her question mark connected
with order and the noble life in the tale, and here she has a point worth
considering. The part may be a compositional failure in overstepping the

mark, but the celebration of the noble life that Muscatine suggested (see p 17) is very hard to verify on the evidence of such narratorial interventions as this, completing an anti-heroic picture of Arcite and Palamon, which has been built up throughout the poem.

There is on the other hand no reason to overdo the importance of the sudden preoccupation with human anatomy. It runs out of control as does the long *occupatio* in lines 2919–66, but the overall narrative control is never threatened. To balance the 'faintly macabre humour',[9] the passage is followed by a truly moving death speech by Arcite, nobly and in the high style reuniting himself with Palamon and taking leave of Emily. When the narrator appears again some 30 lines later the decorous pathos is well and truly established through Arcite's dying words, given in a voice belonging to heroic-epic convention and romance. This is true *gentilesse*, and we see that all the young foolishness is gone. The representational form of narration, showing without commenting, is used most appropriately.

When the narrator regains control of the story it is not to let Arcite ascend to the eighth sphere as in Boccaccio's version. A plausible explanation is that Chaucer had already prepared his version of *Troilus and Criseyde*, for which he used this episode in the great ending. Moreover, the substitution is, as Piero Boitani has pointed out, 'a philosophical and narrative choice' which is 'consistent with his narrative.'[10] As for philosophy, we have seen how the narratorial comments generally reflect a refusal to be high-flown in favour of realistic common sense, and the tone is also very much on a par with the type of humour and self-consciousness that has been displayed so far:

> His spirit chaunged hous and wente ther,
> As I cam nevere, I kan nat tellen wher.
> Therefore I stynte; I nam no divinistre;
> Of soules fynde I nat in this registre,
> Ne me ne list thilke opinions to telle
> Of hem, though that they writen wher they dwelle.
> Arcite is coold, ther Mars his soule gye!
> (2809–15)

The choice of the word 'coold' borders on narratorial cynicism, but on the other hand it echoes the cold and sinister route on which Mars guides Arcite's soul, as indicated in the portrait of Mars in book III. In a brief analysis Boitani traces 'what looks like a system of repeated allusions culminating in one central image,' claiming convincingly that Arcite's 'coold' death has been premonitioned by the series of images associated with the pagan gods.[11] This suggestion will be further explored in chapter 6, but here we may conclude that the apparently cynical humour has a wider significance.

As for the narratorial option not to get involved in divination, this is certainly another of Chaucer's flippancies.[12] The realism and non-involvement in relation to the deeper questions that the poem raises stands in direct opposition to the foregrounding of philosophy and the pagan universe. In other words the narratorial stance in this respect contradicts the narrative design. It becomes a *Riesenscherz* that Chaucer, who himself translated Boethius' *Consolation,* and who in the poem has used material from this and from the equally safe homeground of classical mythology, has chosen to let his narrator disclaim any knowledge of abstract or divine learning. Even more so because, as we shall see, the narrator is in fact highly involved when it comes to philosophical matters and representations of the pagan gods.

## Notes to chapter 5

1. Barbara Nolan, *Chaucer and the Tradition of the Roman Antique* (Cambridge: *Cambridge Studies in Medieval Literature,* 15, 1992), p 271.
2. For a full analysis see Jeffrey Heltermann, 'The Dehumanizing Metamorphoses of the Knight's Tale' in *English Literary History,* 38, 1971.
3. Elisabeth Salter, *Chaucer: The Knight's Tale and the Clerk's Tale* (London: Edward Arnold, 1962), p 25.
4. The examples are from respectively Charles Moseley, ed., *Geoffrey Chaucer: The Knight's Tale* (Harmondsworth: Penguin, 1987), p 57 and Michael Alexander, *York Notes on the Knight's Tale* (Burnt Mill, Harrow, Essex: Longman York Press, 1981, 2nd ed., 1990), p 86.
5. Alexander, p 86.
6. Professor Spearing has pointed out to me that this scientific code of language is in fact a general preoccupation of Chaucer's in *The Canterbury Tales,* 'from *licour* in *General Prologue 3* downwards'. The point is well taken, and it certainly provides *some* explanation for the oddity of the passage. Cf the discussion below.
7. Derek Pearsall, *The Life of Geoffrey Chaucer* (Oxford: Blackwell, 1992), p 158.
8. Kathleen A. Blake, 'Order and the Noble Life in Chaucer's *Knight's Tale?*' in *Modern Language Quarterly,* 34, 1973, 11.
9. This expression is borrowed from F. Anne Payne, *Chaucer and Menippean Satire* (Madison: University of Wisconsin Press, 1981), p 252. She refers to 'faintly macabre Menippean humor, which depends on a dislocating shift in point of view.' I take the liberty to use the phrase without endorsing the interpretation of *The Knight's Tale* as Menippean satire. See further my comments to Payne's analysis in chapter 2.

10. Piero Boitani, 'What Dante meant to Chaucer' in Boitani, ed., *Chaucer and the Italian Trecento* (Cambridge: Cambridge University Press, 1983), p 126.
11. Boitani, 'Style, Iconography and Narrative' in *ibid.*, p 197.
12. The word 'flippancies' is borrowed from Paul Strohm's discussion of Arcite's death. Strohm, it should be added, applies these to the Knight-narrator. See *Social Chaucer* (Cambridge: Harvard University Press, 1989), p 133.

CHAPTER 6

# Seriousness, High Style, Involvement:
# The Pagan Deities

I have claimed earlier that the descriptive passages in book III show Chaucer at his most innovative. Certainly book III has the largest quantity of passages that find no equivalent in Bocaccio's *Teseida*, although Chaucer has reduced the action to a bare minimum compared to Boccaccio's longwinded representation of the preliminaries before the great tournament and the arrival of the participants (books 6–7). Rather than innovations in the storyline (the only major change being a separation of the prayers of the lovers from the descriptions of the temples), Chaucer has amplified the descriptions significantly and added the episode with the gods at the end of the book. There is clearly inspiration from *The Romance of the Rose*, notably in some allegorical passages (1925–41, 1996–8, 2009–12, 2028–30), and the description of Venus seems to have been drawn partly from Bersuire's *Ovidius Moralizatus*. Besides, some resemblances to Statius' *Thebaid* have been traced by various critics.[1] However, the poetic organization is entirely Chaucer's, the poetry representing perhaps more than any other parts of the tale a *tour de force*.[2] Critical reactions to the temple scenes have characteristically included adjectives such as 'grisly', 'dehumanising', 'destructive', 'horrific', 'heartless', and 'unpleasant'.[3] Such strong evaluations are entirely justified because of the forceful imagery, the vivid details and the poetic sound qualities, particularly in the depictions of the temples of Mars, Venus and Diana. Before turning to a close analysis of this passage, however, let us consider its context in the poem and its background in Chaucer's poetry.

After the narrator's self-conscious display of concern about proper decorum (see also chapter 4, p 70), he turns to a description of Theseus' 'noble theatre' (1885). This is given in the high style of rhetoric, as suggested by the frame of reference in words like 'roially' (1884), 'noble' (1884, 1913, 1915), 'marbul' (1893), 'gold' (1908), 'coral' (1910) and 'riche' (1911). The tone of voice corresponds largely to Boccaccio's in its enthusiasm for pomp, but the narrator again refuses to let himself be carried away and breaks off after some thirty lines, following the line from his *abbrevatio*– formula in line 1895, 'And shortly for to concluden'. What now follows is still a description, but the narrative form is significantly different from the *Teseida*.

At first sight the reader may well be puzzled by the direct address 'maystow se' in line 1918, even more so because a continued repetition of 'saugh I' (2011, 2017, 2028, 2062, 2067 and 2073) indicates the narrator's literal presence in his own third-person story. David Lawton, cited at the beginning of chapter 2, is obviously right in pointing to a discrepancy between the ostensible narrator and the 'I' speaking here, and anyone asserting that the Knight is the narrator will have to come to terms with the problem presented by this discrepancy. The frequent repetition of the 'saugh I'-formula speaks against a simple slip of the kind we find in *The Shipman's Tale*, where the 'we' and 'us' at the beginning of the tale suggest a female speaker (VII, 12, 14, 18, 19). We may perhaps best talk about an inconsistency which Chaucer himself would not have considered at all, exactly because he is not worried about the fiction of a Knight-narrator. Understandably very few of the critics operating with a persona comment on the 'saugh I'-formula, and most of those that do resort to the idea that the Knight becomes so involved with his material that he gets carried away and gives an eyewitness account of something that he will have experienced in warfare. Lee Patterson is one of the recent critics to hold this view, and in fact he employs it as a central point in his interpretation of the tale and the 'undoing' of the Knight's narration.[4]

The impression of a narrator who gets carried away is understandable, since the voice in this description of the temples is both intense and involved. The combination of the first and second person with forms of the verb 'see' adds intimacy to the stark visual quality of the presentation. It is, however, not a case of the Knight losing control of the story; what we have is Chaucer the poet in full control of a *visio*. The distance of the realistic narrator disappears, and the Chaucerian voice so characteristic of his early poetry takes over. We will have to be satisfied with an explanation on the lines that Chaucer was apparently more interested in what he felt to be the proper poetic code than in consistency of narration. And the code for a dream vision was one particularly well known to him. Not only had he become familiar with it in his translation of *The Romance of the Rose*, he also employed it in three major poems of his own that were written before *The Knight's Tale*.

In *The Book of the Duchess* the fiction of a dream is elegantly used as a framing device (framing lines 291–1323), partly to obtain decorous distance to the delicate story-matter, partly to evoke the conventional romance setting for the dreamer's encounter with the black knight. As in *The Knight's Tale* gods and goddesses as well as other figures from classical antiquity crop up as the dreamer moves on, and also here we get a *visio* of paintings on a wall:

> And alle the walles with colours fyne
> Were peynted, bothe text and glose,
> Of al the Romaunce of the Rose.
> (*The Book of the Duchess*, 332–4)

Thus directly, and conveniently, does Chaucer acknowledge his most direct inspiration.

*The House of Fame* again has the main story framed as a dream vision, the frame itself being formally structured as proems and invocations at the beginning of each book. Chaucerian playfulness and overt narratorial self-consciousness at times almost spoil the fiction for the sake of realistic comedy, as when the eagle continues to put the naive 'Geffrey' (729) right in the debate that takes up book II, having woken him up actually *within* the dream in a voice 'That useth oon I koude nevene.' (562) Presumably a homely allusion to Chaucer's wife, a wonderful joke being played on their archetypal man-and-wife relationship:

> For hyt was goodly seyd to me
> *So nas hyt never wont to be.*
> (*The House of Fame*, 565–6, my italics)

Jocularity dominates *The House of Fame* and gives it a different mode of voice from *The Knight's Tale*. In the actual *visio*– parts, ie the passages regarding the dreamer's (conventionally) fantastic visions, there are on the other hand striking parallels to the seriousness, high style and involvement of the temple scenes in *The Knight's Tale*:

> First saugh I the destruction
> Of Troye thurgh the Grek Synon,
> ...
> And next that sawgh I how Venus,

Whan that she sawgh the castel brende
Doun fro the heven gan descende,
...
Ther saugh I such tempeste aryse
That every herte myght agryse
To see hyt peynted on the wal
(*The House of Fame*, 151–2, 162–4, 209–11)

These are excerpts from the *visio* of the temple of Venus with the same kind of destructive images painted on the wall and with the identical formula of 'saugh I', in fact repeated all through this part. The poetic force and tight structure of the later poem is not yet there, but technically Chaucer shows his skills at least in glimpses, as indicated by these examples. This is also so in *The Parliament of Fowls*. Another parallel scene has the dreamer in this poem pass through the dark temple of Venus ('Derk was that place, but afterward lightnesse/ I saw a lyte ..., 263–4). The *visio* here has many echoes from the pleasant garden in *The Romance of the Rose*, and the tone is distinctly light, although we get this dark image of Venus and also a reminder of one destructive aspect of love:

Withinne the temple, of sykes hoote as fyr
I herde a swogh that gan aboute renne,
Which sikes were engendered with desyr,
That maden every auter for to brenne
Of new flaume; and wel espyed I thenne
That al the cause of sorwes that they drye
Cam of the bittere goddesse Jelosye.
(*The Parliament of Fowls*, 246–52)

We may conclude that Chaucer has practised well in the tradition of 'literary pictorialism or iconic poetry' before attempting his artistically most complete and original *visio* in *The Knight's Tale*.[5]

Analysing the long *visio* of lines 1918–2088 from the point of view of narration has become a much easier task after Barbara Nolan's recent in-depth study of Chaucer and the *roman antique*. Before adding some observations I will consider Nolan's excellent discussion of the passage at some length, starting with two quotations that establish an important starting point:

> For all the display of wealth and craft in the paintings, it would be difficult to imagine grimmer galleries of art than those invented by Chaucer for Theseus' temples.

> Chaucer, by contrast, widens the scope of the destruction, misfortune, and pain he aligns with Mars, Venus and Diana, and he discourages allegorization.[6]

In stressing the grimness of the iconographic details, Nolan also points to the celebration of magnificence in the art, and she shows how Chaucer deliberately changes the focus away from allegory and towards the images of disorder and destruction. In other words Chaucer operates on a grand scale and at the same time directs the pattern of visual effects towards the darker powers of pagan divinities. Nolan's main argument is that

> we confront metonymically in the *matere* of Theseus' wall paintings ... the same pattern of destructive *aventure*, mischance and passion that governs the Tale.
> (P. 275, Nolan's italics)

This is supported by an analysis that shows how Chaucer's images emphasize the human victims rather than the divine agents of misery and continually portray the apparent meaninglessness and accidental nature of the pagan world. She links this analysis with what she sees as the poem's 'Stoically defined world', which offers no Christian consolation of philosophy. A crucial point, which will be considered again in my discussion of the philosophical passages in chapter 7.

Turning to the passage itself, I will try to enlarge the scope of Nolan's argument by applying close reading and adding further commentary. In the temple of Venus the victims of love are portrayed first:

> The broken slepes, and the sikes colde
> The sacred teeris, and the waymentynge,
> The firy strokes of the desirynge
> That loves servantz in this lyf enduren
> The othes that hir covenantz assuren
> (1920–24)

These images describe such destructive passion as we have seen in the love of Palamon and Arcite, as Nolan correctly suggests. If we take the passage quite literally, it might in fact also be seen as a brief catalogue of elements in the poem's main story: the broken sleep, the tears, wailing and desire, and more particularly broken oaths, have all been represented as characteristic of the miserable universe of love (cf the discussion in chapter 3). The brief list of allegorical personifications, moving in the next four lines from 'Plesaunce' to 'Jalosye' can equally be seen as representative of elements directly present in the tale itself, stressing again destructive forces in love. The 'ensamples' take us away from this list of reminders but lend the same general impression, eg 'The riche Cresus, haytyf in servage' (1946). However, the narrator's enthusiastic voice steps in to reassure us that there is also another side to Venus:

> Festes, instrumentz, caroles, daunces,
> Lust and array, and alle the circumstaunces
> Of love, which that I rekned and rekne shal,
> (1931–3)

The narrator is apparently struggling to achieve a more nuanced balance in the representation of love, but in the context the destructive images are so dominant that they are in fact only strengthened by contrast. Once again there is ambivalence in the narrative design, but the foreshadowing of a tragic outcome is becoming increasingly conspicuous.

The temple of Mars, which is to be the scene for Arcite's prayer, reinforces the ominous perspective of his fate. To Nolan's point about destructive *aventure* may be added that the direction the poem is taking is from now on quite unambiguous. The horrible powers of Mars are rendered almost without narratorial intervention besides the conventional 'saugh I'-formula, and the visual impact of showing without commenting becomes the most forceful in the poem. The metonymic technique takes us through a series of related images, starting in a carefully drawn portrayal of the temple of Mars in its waste land setting (1967–94), then moving on to a 'derke ymaginyng' of images under Martian domain (1995–2040), finally to depict the statue of Mars (2041–50).

In the first of these parts the barrenness of the 'colde, frosty regioun' (1973) is evoked through the image of an empty forest

> With knotty, knarry, bareyne trees olde,
> Of stubbes sharpe and hidouse to biholde,

In which ther ran a rumbel in a swough,
As though a storm sholde bresten every bough.
(1977–80)

It is lines such as these with their tough alliterative sounds and the synaesthetic mixture of sound and vision which must have appealed so strongly to T. S. Eliot as he created his own great modern *Waste Land*.[7] Unlike some commentators (see note to these lines in *The Riverside Chaucer*), Eliot will have been able to appreciate the mixture of sound and vision in this dark poetic painting. The synaesthesia is carried on to the image of 'Mars armypotente' (1982), from which comes 'a rage and swich a veze/ That it made al the gate for to rese' (1985–6). We can almost feel the gate shaking in this dramatically rendered experience, and in the following lines we are drawn further into the faintly lit temple, invited through the iron door alongside the narrator. The iron bars and the fortified pillars create a horrible sense of imprisonment.

In this setting is displayed a second cluster of visions, now in the form of one- or two-liners evoking the most terrible nightmares of the human imagination:

The crueel Ire, reed as any gleede;
The pykepurs, and eek the pale Drede;
The smylere with the knyf under the cloke;
The shepne brennynge with the blake smoke;
The tresoun of the mordrynge in the bedde,
The open werre, with woundes al bibledde;
(1997–2002)

The list continues almost endlessly. As Richard Neuse remarks in a comparison with Dante's *Inferno*, the narrator 'takes on the air of a Dantean tourist in hell,' only he need not descend into the otherworld, since he leaves the impression that 'hell is ... where the pagan gods are.'[8] This is particularly true of the temple of Mars, because there are no images working contrary to our dominant impression.

'Ire' and 'Drede' are among a few allegorical figures referred to in this part, along with for instance 'Meschaunce' and 'Woodnesse' in the following lines. However, Nolan is right in observing that the allegorical personifications so characteristic of *The Romance of the Rose*-type *visio* are less conspicuous here. Maybe Chaucer realised the stronger effects of his 'ensamples', with which he masterfully pinpoints typesituations and draws icons that are horrendous because they are so specific. Lines 1992–2000 are examples of that, and few readers of *The Knight's Tale* will have failed to notice, even after a single perusal, such lines as these and also

> The hunte strangled with the wilde beres;
> The sowe freten the child right in the cradel;
> ...
> The cartere overryden with his carte –
> Under the wheel ful lowe he lay adoun.
> (2018–19 and 2022–3)

This is worse than a modern horror film and not surpassed by anything in Chaucer's own work as far as visual power is concerned. The half insane nature of this dark vision is underlined by a simile in the description of the statue of Mars, about whom it says that he 'looked grym as he were wood'. The cruel, anti-human identity of Mars is furthermore laid bare in a final image, grossly contradictive of the Martian 'glorie' invoked in the last line of the portrait (2050):

> A wolf ther stood biforn hym at his feet
> With eyen rede, and of a man he eet;
> (2047–8)

This is the second image of man-eating (cf line 2019) and a third completes this small chain in the description of Diana's temple. Here we get Ovid's story from the *Metamorphoses* of the unfortunate Actaeon, who was eaten by his own dogs after being changed into a hart. (2065–8) In the representation of the last temple the line from the other two descriptions is followed, but it is as if Chaucer at this point has felt that enough is enough. At any rate he has the narrator interrupt after only a few examples, remarking before these that 'As shortly as I kan, I wol me haste' (2052) and afterwards:

> Ther saugh I many other wonder storie,
> The which me list nat to drawen to memorie.
> (2073–4)

The narratorial impatience seems quite appropriate at this point and it imposes limits for and control of the *visio*, which now ends with a brief iconographic portrait of the goddess Diana herself. The final image evoked here, that of an unborn child and a woman in labour crying for pity, leaves us with a strong parallel to central motifs in the poem: Imprisonment in life and the merciless gods.

After an interval of very little action and much more description, albeit in a much brighter key, follows a parallel sequence to the temple scene. This episode renders the prayers of Palamon, Emily, and Arcite to each of the deities introduced at the beginning of the book. As Pearsall notes, Chaucer has taken elaborate care 'to observe the infiltration of astrological significances' into his account as each prayer takes place at the appropriate hour when each planet is in a propitious constellation.[9] Generally speaking the prayers are made in high rhetoric and with extreme dedication and sincerity of voice, in the narrator's words respectively 'with humble cheere' (2219), 'with pitous cheere' (2295) and 'with pitous herte and heigh devocioun' (2371). In the introductions to the prayers the narrator's strategy is clearly to make the audience forget for a while the sinister tone of the earlier descriptions. After all, as Salter observes, these were 'only *painted* terrors'.[10] Now the images of the gods are slightly more benign, and the setting has shifted from the barren waste land to an early, sunny morning with bird song. Venus is here 'honourable and digne' (2216), Diana is rather neutrally drawn, and even Mars is only 'fierse' (2369). Still the awesome attitudes of all three petitioners support the earlier impression that they are 'unwitting pawns in the hands of greater powers', as Jill Mann has phrased it.[11]

In the first prayer Palamon says to Venus:

> Allas! I ne have no langage to telle
> Th'effects ne the tormentz of myn helle;
> (2227–8)

Yet language of proper decorum is exactly what Chaucer has given to him and to Arcite, and the modesty formula is all part of the rhetorical code. Poetically Chaucer is elegant even in such a stylistically conventional form, as we see for instance in the smooth flow of Palamon's invocation (2221–6). It is delightfully simplistic ('Fairest of faire, O lady myn, Venus') and includes the most pathetic of all rhyme pairs in medieval complaints, 'smerte' and 'herte', yet it safely brings home the message of religious devotion. Palamon, like later Arcite, is here shown to be ennobled and matured through love:

> Ne I ne axe nat tomorwe to have victorie,
> Ne renoun in this cas, ne veyne glorie
> (2239–40)

Palamon's humble position and honest sincerity certainly shows a development from the ignoble behaviour in the grove-episode, and the narrative voice, it seems, is preparing us for a grand finale. Also there is a suspense element inherent in the situation: How can both lovers be granted what they pray for?

Emily's prayer is squeezed in between the more significant petitions of the two lovers, and in fact this is the only time she is given any individual characteristics beyond romance convention. The long descriptive part that precedes her prayer is purely conventional, apart from the odd and rather coarse narratorial comment mentioned in chapter 5 (2284–8), and Emily's prayer 'to ben a mayden al my lyf' adds little to her character, but serves more to illustrate Diana's role as the goddess of chastity. However, in her reaction to the vehement and dramatic answer that the goddess gives to her prayer, Emily is given some presence of flesh and blood.[12] She is very human in her initial response:

> For which so soore agast was Emelye
> That she was wel ny mad and gan to crye,
> (2341–2)

It is here that the narrator steps in to appeal directly for pity. (2345) A bit later Emily is shown as 'astoned', and she asks a personal question that on a smaller scale echoes Palamon's grand question to the gods in book I (1313–14): 'What amounteth this, allas?' (2362) The narrator leaves the question to raise the level of suspense, and he leaves Emily with sympathetic understanding of a kind that may be inconsistent with the general detachment from the characters, but which can be explained by Chaucer's general attitude towards women. It is hard to find any portrait of women in Chaucer's works that does not at some point include this kind of narratorial intervention to evoke sympathy. In terms of communicative theory, there are always *upgraders*.

Arcite's prayer is represented in a parallel, almost symmetrical structure to Palamon's. The attitude and rhetoric is also quite similar, but of course the conflict between Venus and Mars is stressed, notably by the short version of his early poem *The Complaint of Mars*, which Chaucer has inserted in lines 2383–90. The result of the structural design is a sense of power balance between the two forces, and even though Palamon and Arcite are now champion knights of Venus and Mars, and Arcite is given the epithet 'the stronge' (2421), it is still difficult to distinguish their characters. The images of the pagan gods are clearly foregrounded, reducing the knights to simple tools in their game of war:

> And right anon swich strif ther is bigonne,
> For thilke grauntyng, in the hevene above,
> Bitwixe Venus, the godesse of love,
> And Mars, the stierne god armypotente,
> (2438–41)

Here is the perspective from which Chaucer now invites us to view the story. Compared to the *Teseida* the argument in heaven carries more weight, partly because the figure of Saturn is introduced in this episode, partly because it is placed at the end of the book which has had the pagan universe as its central frame of reference. A closer inspection of Saturn's influence and the function of this last scene with the pagan deities is required. Here I will refer first of all to a recent extensive critical treatment of Saturn and of this episode in particular, Brown and Butcher's in *The Age of Saturn*.[13] The main point of their study is to show how Chaucer employs the tradition of Saturn and his children to dominate the universe of the tale. The fatal influence of this deity is evoked at an early stage by both Arcite and Palamon (1087 and 1328), and in the episode at the end of book III it becomes clear that Saturn's malevolence will be a determining force. The tradition, and in particular its iconographic details, is convincingly analysed by Brown and Butcher to provide a framework of understanding in a field that was neglected for many years after Curry's classic study.[14] However much I sympathize with Brown and Butcher's *general* assessment of Saturnian influence, I will nevertheless have to disagree with them on many specific points of interpretation.

I have elsewhere discussed Brown and Butcher's highly dubious readings of Chaucerian texts as contemporary political allegory,[15] and my protests to their analysis of Saturn's role are of a similar nature. At several points they apply general characteristics of Saturn to something very specific, and this attempt to make things fit is less than convincing. To give a few examples, I refer first to page 216, in which the iconographic details sometimes evoked about Saturn's children as 'canny with money', and engaged in 'arduous manual labour', are said to be reflected in Arcite as Philostrate. These are characteristics turned upside down in Arcite's case, as he remains a noble knight in his deeds and esteem (1429–50). On page 215 Brown and Butcher are hesitant to interpret the 'cherles rebellyng' of line 2459 as a reference to the Peasants Revolt of 1381, and instead give the far less likely suggestion that besides unrest in late medieval England, it could also refer to 'social upheaval' in *The Knight's Tale* itself. The tyranny of Creon that they mention as an example is absolutely marginal in the tale, and although there is plenty of upheaval, it is hardly *social*. Other parallels, between iconographic details in medieval art depicting Saturn and descriptions in the tale, are cited to demonstrate how 'Saturn's influence spreads to all reaches of the narrative, and to all participants' (p 221), but evidence for such a complete dominance is very scarce indeed, or founded on very conventional iconographic features. For instance Brown and Butcher see the frequency of the colour black as a sign of Saturnian influence, whereas this might simply indicate the predominantly dark mood of the poem (pp 218–19).

Rather than 'spreading to all reaches' of the tale, Saturn's influence is characteristic of the pagan deities in general. In fact the images that Saturn uses to describe himself are strongly reminiscent of the temple scenes earlier in book III:

Myn is the drenchyng in the see so wan;
Myn is the prison in the derke cote;
Myn is the stranglyng and hangyng by the throte,
(2456–8)

The horror of the earlier part is reinvoked and ends book III on an extremely ominous note, although Saturn finds a solution to stop the argument in heaven.

That Saturn is only part of the malevolent pagan universe is supported by respectively Neuse and Burrow in their analyses of the three ages of man. They both establish a structural parallel between heaven and earth, in which youth is represented by Arcite, Palamon and Emily below and by Mars, Venus and Diana above. In the mature age Theseus is matched by

Jupiter in heaven, and in old age the figure of Egeus corresponds to Saturn.[16] Saturn is the old wise figure (2443–8), who has benevolent sides, as have the other pagan gods, but in the tale his disposition is mainly evil. As we learn in Chaucer's own *Treatise of the Astrolabe*, there are several 'wicked' planets, 'as Saturne or Mars or elles the Tayl of the Dragoun' (II, 4, 35–6).

In sum, the narrative design in book III points to the fatal outcome of the story by a forceful poetic depiction of the pagan universe in its darker aspects. In the next chapter we shall trace the pagan influence on the philosophical questions raised in the poem, still focusing on the narrative voice and strategy behind the representation of philosophy. However, it would be worthwhile first to consider Chaucer's own view of this for him so fascinating pagan world:

> Natheles these ben observaunces of judicial matere and rytes of payens, in whiche my spirit hath no feith, ...
> (*A Treatise on the Astrolabe*, II, 4, 57–9)

Chaucer, here commenting on the unfortunate dispositions of stars and planets, finds no faith in pagan matters. He has faith in a religion not known to Palamon and Arcite.

## Notes to chapter 6

1. For a comprehensive discussion of source influences see V. J. DiMarco's explanatory notes in Benson, gen. ed., *The Riverside Chaucer*.
2. This expression is applied to the whole of *The Knight's Tale* by Derek Pearsall in *The Canterbury Tales* (London: Allen and Unwin, 1985), p 129.
3. The first three adjectives are cited from David Aers, *Chaucer* (Brighton: Harvester New Readings, 1986), p 26; the next three in turn from Elisabeth Salter, *Chaucer: The Knight's Tale and the Clerk's Tale* (London: Edward Arnold, 1962), pp 25–27, A. C. Spearing, ed., *The Knight's Tale* (Cambridge: Cambridge University Press, 1966), p 60 and Charles Moseley, ed., *Geoffrey Chaucer: The Knight's Tale* (Harmondsworth: Penguin, 1987), p 56.
4. Lee Patterson, *Chaucer and the Subject of History* (London: Routledge, 1991). See especially p 169 and pp 225–6. Against Patterson's view see also Salter, *Fourteenth-Century English Poetry: Contexts and Readings* (Oxford: Clarendon Press, 1983), p 161. Salter concludes that Chaucer 'loses touch with the fiction of the Knight-narrator (a fiction never particularly strong for him).' She also suggests that the 'saugh I'-formula may be inspired by Boccaccio's *vivedi*.
5. The phrase is Charles Muscatine's in his note to lines 230–94 of *The Parliament of Fowls* in *The Riverside Chaucer*. This note also traces the tradition back to Homer via Boccaccio, Dante, Fasti, Ovid and Virgil.

6. Barbara Nolan, *Chaucer and the Tradition of the Roman Antique* (Cambridge: *Cambridge Studies in Medieval Literature*, 15, 1992), pp 272–8. The first two quotations are from p 274.

7. T. S. Eliot's admiration was at any rate outspoken, as also indicated by his many oblique references to Chaucer. (Even the first line of *The Waste Land*, 'April is the cruellest month breeding' echoes the beginning of *The Canterbury Tales*). There is of course no direct reference from Eliot to the lines cited here, but the general parallel seems to justify my speculation.

8. Richard Neuse, *Chaucer's Dante: Allegory and Epic Theater in The Canterbury Tales* (Berkeley and L. A.: University of California Press, 1991), p 124. Neuse claims that the Knight as narrator is 'wholly unmoved by the horror and absurdity' of the descriptions, and here it will appear that I disagree: There is no Knight-persona here, and the disappearance of narratorial commentary is a deliberate choice to enhance the visual effect. However, the comparison with Dante's *Inferno* is entirely appropriate.

9. Pearsall 1985, p 129.

10. Salter, *Chaucer: The Knight's Tale and the Clerk's Tale*, p 27.

11. Jill Mann, 'The Planetary Gods in Chaucer and Henryson' in Ruth Morse and Barry Windeatt, eds., *Chaucer Traditions: Studies in Honour of Derek Brewer* (Cambridge: Cambridge University Press, 1990), p 94.

12. In his article 'The Masculine Narrator and Four Women of Style' E. Talbot Donaldson reaches the following interesting conclusion about Emily:

> When Palamon first saw her he mistook her for a goddess; but I'm not sure that Arcite was not even more mistaken in supposing that she was a woman. She deceived them both, for she was only an idea, though one of more importance to the idea of chivalry than a real woman could have been.

Reprinted in Donaldson, *Speaking of Chaucer* (London: The Athlone Press, University of London, 1970), p 50. As indicated earlier, I agree that Emily is *mainly* represented as a passive stereotype, but the prayer scene is an exception.

13. Peter Brown and Andrew Butcher, *The Age of Saturn* (Oxford: Basil Blackwell, 1991). In what follows all page numbers refer to the part 'The influence of Saturn' in the chapter on the Knight.

14. Walter Clyde Curry, *Chaucer and the Medieval Sciences* (London: Oxford University Press, 1926, 2nd revised edition, New York: Barnes & Noble, 1960).

15. See Klitgård, 'Chaucer and Modern Criticism' in *Engelsk Meddelelser*, 1993.

16. Richard Neuse, 'The Knight: The First Mover in Chaucer's Human Comedy' in *University of Toronto Quarterly*, 31, 1962, and J. A. Burrow, 'Chaucer and the Three Ages of Man in Burrow, ed., *Essays on Medieval Literature* (Oxford: Clarendon Press, 1984).

# CHAPTER 7

# Seriousness, High Style, Involvement: the Philosophical Passages

In the narrative design of *The Knight's Tale* three philosophical passages add further significance to the meaning of the poem's pagan universe. These are integrated in Arcite and Palamon's speeches at the end of book I and in Theseus' speech at the end of book IV, and all are based on material from Boethius' *De Consolatione Philosophiae*. However, Chaucer has taken care to alter important philosophical conclusions from the *Consolation*, or to simply not include these, and the effects of this deliberate narrative strategy will be the main concern of this chapter.

We have already touched upon the narrator's many references to elements of fortune: 'aventure', 'destiny', 'cas' and 'chance' occurring frequently in narratorial comments on changes in the fates of Palamon and Arcite.[1] In this way the agenda is set for an exploration of Lady Fortune's mutability, the narrator adopting a standard explanation for all changes of luck. This is of course very much in the tradition of medieval story-telling and a favourite device in Chaucer's poetic vocabulary, but the idea of the fickleness of Fortune is given further meaning.[2] Besides the integration of the idea with the representation of the destructive pagan gods (see chapter 6), Chaucer has also gone beyond the merely conventional in the philosophical passages. Arcite's statements, 'Wel hath Fortune yturned thee the dys' and 'syn Fortune is chaungable ...' (1238 and 1242) are traditional expressions of complaint, but his third mention of Fortune calls for further attention:

"Allas, why pleynen folk so in commune
On purveiaunce of God, or of Fortune,"
(1251–2)

Strictly speaking 'the purveiaunce of God' is an anachronism, since Arcite lives in a pre-Christian society, but as this is obviously not a problem for

Chaucer and for his contemporaries, let us not worry too much about it.[3] More to the point, Arcite does not distinguish between providence and fate, whereas Chaucer must implicitly have assumed his audience's familiarity with this important distinction. In his translation of the *Consolation* the difference is spelled out:

> And thilke divine thought that is iset and put in the tour (that is to seyn, in the heighte) of the simplicete of God, stablissith many maner gises to thinges that ben to done; the whiche manere whan that men looken it in thilke pure clennesse of the devyne intelligence, it is ycleped purveaunce; but whanne thilke manere is referred by men to thinges that it moeveth and disponyth, than of olde men it was clepyd destyne.
> (*Boece*, IV, pr. 6, 47–56)

The Christian God, it appears, has *foreknowledge* of destiny, a point of much concern in the *Consolation* generally. As is the question of still allowing for man's free will, a favorite subject of debate in the late middle ages.[4] Like Troilus at the end of book IV in *Troilus and Criseyde*, Arcite is not in a position to grasp the nature of providence and of free will, and consequently he becomes deterministic:

> "Syn that I may nat seen you, Emelye,
> I nam but deed; ther nys no remedye."
> (1273–4)

In many ways Arcite is himself like the 'dronke man' he refers to in line 1264, as the Boethian context (*Boece*, 3, pr. 2) makes clear. In an analysis Edward C. Schweitzer has shown how Arcite's speech in this respect is a piece of dramatic irony, since he continually goes astray and fails to seek true felicity.[5] The whole point must be for Chaucer to emphasize by implication that this true felicity lies nowhere short of God, and so Arcite in his pagan setting is left to despair, especially at this early stage of the story. He is yet immature and as we have seen also a victim of juvenile folly, but in fact he never comes fully to terms with his own destiny, even in his noble outcry against the gods on his deathbed:

> What is this world? What asketh men to have?
> Now with his love, now in his colde grave

Allone, withouten any compaignye.
(2777–9)

Chaucer's narrative technique is quite remarkable in the philosophical passages. The narrative voice is hidden, pointing out by means of the Christian, Boethian knowledge shared with the audience that the pagan world lacked the consolation of philosophy – and God's mercy. Palamon's speech in book I is as much a reminder of this lack of mercy, poetically represented in the high style of rhetoric and in lofty, serious language:

Thanne seyde he, "O crueel goddes that governe
This world with byndyng of youre word eterne,
And writen in the table of atthamaunt
Youre parlement and youre eterne graunt,
What is mankynde moore unto you holde
Than is the sheep that rouketh in the folde?"
...

"What governance is in this prescience,
That giltelees tormenteth innocence?"
(1303–8 and 1313–14)

The rest of the poem, especially from book III onwards, gives weight to Palamon's argument, but the hidden narrative voice gives counterweight. Here not only by means of an overall dramatic irony, but also by weaving Christian concepts into the speech: 'prescience', 'innocence' and 'penaunce' (1313–15). Palamon's vision of 'a serpent or a theef' (1325) evokes the Fall of Man, and Chaucer again succeeds in reminding his audience of the ancient setting before the redemption of mankind. His narratorial voice is thus deeply involved in manipulating the speech with Christian symbolism, even though the narrator is technically outside.

The narrator in fact never gets directly involved in any of the serious questions raised in the poem. Chaucer lets him play ignorant, and in a performance situation with a less clear distinction between poet and narrator this must have worked as modest self-irony, even though it is of a less obvious kind than that practised in *Sir Thopas* or *The Tale of Melibee*. 'I nam no divinistre' (2811, see chapter 6) is the most direct disclaimer of responsibility we get concerning the narrator's refusal to enter into a discussion of Christian philosophy and the pagan universe. However, it is at this point of the poem, in connection with Arcite's death in book 4, that the tone again becomes philosophical. The first philosophical statement is short and concise, made by Theseus' father Egeus, the second is much more complicated, Theseus' 'First Mover'-speech.

Egeus is introduced for the first time in the poem and disappears as quickly as he enters. In this respect and in his consolatory function it is fair to compare him to Jupiter (see also chapter 6). The narrator introduces him as one 'that knew this worldes transmutacioun,' (2839) and he is thus opposed to the 'ignorant' narrator himself. The narratorial stance is reverent, as also indicated by the admiration for experience (2840–2) and the praise for Egeus' comforting of the people, 'ful wisely', (2851). It is in this context that we must view his statement, which has so often been scorned in criticism for representing Polonius-like wisdom or mere superficiality:

"Right as ther dyed nevere man," quod he,
"That he ne lyvede in erthe in some degree,
Right so ther lyvede never man," he seyde,
"In al this world, that som tyme he ne deyde.
This world nys but a thurghfare ful of wo,
And we been pilgrymes, passynge to and fro.
Deeth is an ende of every worldly soore."
(2843–9)

The question is of course whether this is meant as philosophy at all. Undeniably it does not compare favourably with, say, Aristotle or Aquinas, but such a comparison is not really relevant. Nor is the comparison with Shakespeare's Polonius. Chaucer's point is instead to evoke an image of transcience through a figure representing the human experience in a pagan world. The image itself is both striking and significant, that of pilgrims passing to and fro in a world full of sorrow. An image casting a bleak perspective on the tale and its universe, but also on a larger scale carrying associations to the pilgrimage of *The Canterbury Tales*. As a contrast, the latter journey has a specific goal rather than the 'to and fro' of the pagan world. And death is not that goal, but only the end of every *worldly* misery.

Theseus' First Mover-speech is marked just as much by its pagan context, as again there can be no Christian consolation. Yet Theseus is the only one in a position to offer the consolation that is possible in the context of the tale. Before studying how he gets away with providing the denouement, let us, however, consider his figure as it is presented both in *The Knight's Tale* itself and elsewhere in Chaucer's poetry.

Theseus is the hero from classical antiquity that Chaucer represented most frequently in his poetry. In *Anelida and Arcite* we meet him briefly as the glorious warlord 'With laurer corouned' (24). He is followed by his men carrying the banner of Mars, but only the splendour and glory in this symbol of victory is mentioned. He leads his wife Hippolyta and her sister Emily in a chariot of gold, and his triumph is unmitigated. The narrator takes leave of 'this noble prince Theseus' after some 25 lines, 'In al the flour of Fortunes yevynge.' (44–5)

The unspotted heroic image is altered significantly in *The Legend of Ariadne*, which relates the most famous story about Theseus, his encounter with the Minotaur in Mino's labyrinth. In this version Theseus is extremely hesitant and asks Ariadne to give him a disguise to save his life (*The Legend of Good Women*, 2029–49). After Ariadne has helped him overcome the minotaur, Theseus in fact breaks his vow of faithfulness to her, 'and as a traytour stal his wey.' (2174) The narrator comments: 'A twenty develway the wynd hym dryve! (2127) and also ends the story with 'the devel quyte hym his while!' (2227)

In *The Legend of Phyllis* Theseus' treachery has already become legendary. Commenting on 'false Demophon' (2398), the narrator adds:

> In love a falser herde I nevere non,
> But if it were his fader Theseus.
> (*The Legend of Good Women*, 2399–2400)

Theseus' false behaviour in love is mentioned three more times in this legend (2445–7, 2464 and 2544–5), and we learn that his glory is a thing of the past:

> For of Athenes duk and lord was he,
> As Theseus his fader hadde be,
> That in his tyme was of gret renoun.
> (2442–4)

What emerges from Chaucer's representation of Theseus outside *The Knight's Tale* is thus an ambivalent image of a great hero with human flaws.

It is on this background that we must consider his figure in the tale, although a long tradition of Chaucer criticism has largely ignored this perspective. Surely Chaucer will have respected the mythology of Theseus as he set out to characterize him in more detail.

In *The Knight's Tale* we meet Theseus at middle age and at the height of his glory. As often noted in criticism, and as indicated in my analysis, his qualities as a military leader and as a ruler are undisputed.[6] The narratorial comments and the laudatory outcries from the people can be cited as evidence. As far as his human qualities are concerned, Theseus does behave nobly in showing mercy to the widows at the beginning of the tale, and later to Palamon and Arcite by twice exempting them from further punishment. Yet we have also seen how Theseus is somewhat rash in his judgement and how his language is at times unchivalric. The episodes mentioned support this impression. When Theseus asks the widows,

> "What folk been ye, that at myn homcomynge
> Perturben so my feste with criynge?"
>
> ... "Have ye so greet envye
> Of myn honour, that thus compleyne and crye?"
> (905–8)

he is far from being gentle. Even though a modern psychological interpretation, judging this as unfeeling and ego-boosting, would be going too far, there does seem little justification for his outcry. Theseus ought to have reacted with more understanding in the first place. In the case of his first intervention on behalf of Arcite it is again not his own initiative that leads to the conditional release, but that of Perotheus. And more clearly, it is Queen Hippolyta and her train of women, not Theseus, that promote the eventual sentence after the fight in the grove. (1748–1825)

When we reach the First Mover-speech we have in other words been given more than a hint that Theseus' main qualities lie in military and political leadership rather than in his knowledge of human nature.[7] The mythological background of his later betrayal certainly does not contradict the image of a flawed personality, and the speech itself reflects the speaker also in this respect. The overall strategy is 'to maken vertu of necessitee' (3042), and little else matters. Michael Alexander has the following eloquent comments on Theseus and his speech:

> Symbolically, therefore, Theseus represents the magisterial authority
> of wisdom over the passions ...

> His 'philosophy' here may amount to little more than the necessity
> to make the best of things – a wisdom for which Boethius is not
> necessary.[8]

Indeed Theseus continually subdues the passions in favour of political
wisdom. Thus his speech amounts to a practical arrangement and fails to
offer real consolation.

It starts off in a serious tone and in the high style, describing 'the first
Moevere' and 'the faire cheyne of love' (2987–93). the Boethian argument
continues for some fifty lines, but the style changes to a lower key:

> Wel may men knowe, but it be a fool,
> ...
> ... speces of thynges and progressiouns
> Shullen enduren by successiouns,
> And nat eterne, withouten any lye.
> This maystow understonde and seen at ye.
> (3005, 3013–16)

This is the down-to-earth explanatory style which we also recognize in the
narrator. In this instance, however, the explanation is drawn out unneces-
sarily, and the conclusion is the very practical one in line 3041–2 of
making virtue of necessity. It hardly matches the preceding loftiness.

The remaining part of the speech is directed against 'grucching', a word
mentioned three times (3045, 3058 and 3062). Theseus' argument is that
since Arcite died 'in his excellence and flour' (3048) there is no reason to
keep on mourning: 'But after wo I rede us to be merye'. (3068) As
Theseus says, Arcite cannot thank them, anyway. A final official declara-
tion in the speech prepares for the wedding of Palamon and Emily.

Elisabeth Salter argues convincingly that the assurance of Theseus'
speech is deceptive, and that the conclusion is brisk. Furthermore,

> ...only the confident flow of the poetry disguises the basic illogicality
> of the appeals. The whole affair is put at lowest rating when we are
> told that grief is useless since Arcite is now beyond gratitude –[9]

So what starts as highflown philosophy soon moves on to pragmatism and ends without real consolation. However, Salter is right in pointing to the flow of the poetry as a binding element in Theseus' speech. Apparently Chaucer has wanted to stress the illusion of a deeply philosophical ring to Theseus' words, while at the same time ironically undermining them with the obvious changes to the Boethian argument. The poem leaves its central questions unresolved, even though the narrator tells us that Palamon and Emily live happily ever after. The question of Christian consolation is left to be thematically pursued throughout *The Canterbury Tales* and to be provided only in the very last tale, *The Parson's Tale*.

This is not to say that *The Knight's Tale* should be interpreted solely in allegorical terms, as basically concerned only with the lack of Christian charity. In turning against such a 'Robertsonian' interpretation, Derek Pearsall has argued that Chaucer 'felt an obligation to resist the importunacy of the message of Christian consolation' in representing a pagan universe.[10] Even though the Christian message is implicitly part of the narrative design, it is certainly true that the tale is primarily a fascinating account of a deeply touching – and disturbing – pagan story from Chaucer's classical archives. The pagan world has its limits, as we are shown, but also, despite Theseus' efforts to subdue these, 'ennobling and intense passions', as Wordsworth observed (see p 15). Barbara Nolan has called the tale 'a noble, steadying vision of the passing scene, and a sober, cheerful acceptance of the "necessitee" of change, chance, *aventure*, and death,' stressing the Stoic virtues of the central characters.[11] The narrative design foregrounds the Stoic values, as they are expressed by Arcite, Palamon, Egeus and Theseus in their philosophical (or more accurately philosophizing) speeches, but the narrative voice shows their inadequacy. It is remarkable that this demonstration is achieved most poignantly in the philosophical passages and in the representations of the pagan gods, the narrator having pleaded ignorance of both fields. And this is the great narrative paradox: at the most marked narratorial distance, Chaucer's focus is the sharpest.

# Notes to chapter 7

1. See further the discussion of Barbara Nolan's analysis in chapter 6. The relevant line numbers in *The Knight's Tale* are 1074, 1189, 1235, 1240–3, 1285–90, 1465–6, 1516, 1663–9, 2722.
2. The best comprehensive study of Chaucer's use of the tradition is still Joseph J. Mogan Jr., *Chaucer and the Theme of Mutability* (The Hague and Paris: Mouton, 1969).
3. Such anachronisms occur frequently in Chaucer's works, and in Arcite and Palamon's speeches there are two more examples, 'Got woot' in line 1282 and 'For Goddes sake' in line 1317. The most remarkable anachronisms of this kind in contemporary literature occur in the Old Testament mystery plays, which frequently refer to God, Christ, etc.
4. It is beyond the scope of this thesis to discuss the important philosophical questions at any great length, and general commentaries on medieval philosophy are available in abundance. The essential points about Chaucer's Boethius are covered in Jill Mann, 'Chance and Destiny in *Troilus and Criseyde* and *The Knight's Tale*,' in Boitani and Mann, eds., *The Cambridge Chaucer Companion* (Cambridge: Cambridge University Press, 1986). A more extensive treatment is Bernard L. Jefferson, *Chaucer and the Consolation of Philosophy of Boethius* (Princeton: Princeton University Press, 1973). I have treated the subject in my MA thesis, *Chaucer's Knight's Tale: An Analysis with Special Reference to Theme and Philosophy* (unpublished MA thesis, University of York, 1984).
5. Edward C. Scweitzer, 'Fate and Freedom in *The Knight's Tale*' in *Studies in the Age of Chaucer*, 3, 1981, 31–3.
6. The most influential analysis of Theseus is still Muscatine's in 'Form, Texture and Meaning in Chaucer's *Knight's Tale*' in *Publications of the Modern Language Association of America*, LXV, 1950. See also A. C. Spearing, ed., *The Knight's Tale* (Cambridge: Cambridge University Press, 1966), pp 75–9, for a fine analysis of Theseus and his First Mover-speech. For a challenging and very critical view see David Aers, *Chaucer* (Brighton: Harvester Readings, 1986), chapter 2.
7. Jill Mann's recent view of Theseus as 'the fullest development of an ideal of feminised masculinity' in *Geoffrey Chaucer* (Hemel Hampstead: Harvester Wheatsheaf, *Feminist Readings*, 1991), p 171, is one that I cannot endorse. Indeed I see Theseus as arch-masculine.
8. Michael Alexander, *York Notes on the Knight's Tale* (Burnt Mill, Harrow, Essex: Longman York Press, 1981, 2nd ed., 1990), p 77 and p 85.
9. Elisabeth Salter, *Chaucer: The Knight's Tale and The Clerk's Tale* (London: Edward Arnold, 1962), pp 34–35.
10. Derek Pearsall, *The Life of Geoffrey Chaucer* (Oxford: Blackwell, 1992), p 264.
11. Barbara Nolan, *Chaucer and the Tradition of the Roman Antique* (Cambridge: Cambridge Studies in Medieval Literature, 15, 1992), p 281.

# Conclusion and Summary of Evidence

The end of chapter 7 outlines the main conclusion to this study, explaining the 'paradoxical sense of distance and closeness, of alienation and involvement, of apparent objectivity and myopically close focus' (Pearsall, see p 45). A summary of evidence will establish a fuller basis for a more detailed assessment of Chaucer's narrative voice in *The Knight's Tale*. The summary will lead on to questions of interpretation and a perspective on Chaucer's narrative technique in general.

The hypothesis put forward in the introduction was that rhetorical and stylistic considerations must be at the centre of analysis, and that a comparative angle on especially Chaucer's own works and his direct sources would provide the most accurate context for an evaluation of narrative methods and strategies. My critical approach is stated more precisely in chapter 1. Firstly through a review of the tradition of Chaucer criticism, secondly in an attempt to place Chaucer's narration in a literary communication model by means of recent narrative theory, combined with an investigation of Chaucer's own view of his role as an author.

Two kinds of fallacies in modern approaches to Chaucer are established: the prevailing 20th century tendency to focus on character psychology, irony and persona-narration on the one hand, and the assumption that the text can be regarded without concern for its author on the other. Literary schools such as New Criticism, structuralism, and postmodernism are shown to have provided useful terminology, yet also to be oriented so much towards the novel and other modern genres that a rigid application on medieval literature is not possible. A more extreme conclusion is tentatively that the same problems can be found in the various strongly ideological approaches to Chaucer in this century: the allegorical school, Marxist and Freudian criticism, and to some extent also New Historicism have all proved to be reductive approaches, especially when applied rigidly.

Having dismissed both sustained irony and sustained ideological or methodological focus as the keys to studying Chaucer, let me stress that I do advocate concern for the method of analysis. Structuralist narrative theories such as Chatman's can in fact be adopted for the study of Chaucer's texts, as long as we accept some important reservations in operating with a model for literary communication. What Chaucer will have felt or thought is not the relevant question and may at best lead to entertaining qualified guesses of the kind that we find in literary criticism from the last century. It is, however, extremely relevant to ask where we find Chaucer in relation to his texts, since medieval concepts of text production were so very different from modern ideas. A major result of modern scholarship on medieval theories of authorship, especially the work of Alistair Minnis, has been the clarification of the authorial role. As opposed to later periods, the author is *directly* responsible for his text – ultimately to God (cf the *causa finalis*). I have demonstrated how Chaucer in all his three major works, *Troilus and Criseyde*, *The Legend of Good Women* and *The Canterbury Tales*, proves to be highly aware of his responsibilities as an author, both as creator/translator and as potential poet–performer. Technically we do well in counting the examples rendered in chapter 1 as spoken by Chaucerian narrators, but the implied authors behind these all share the characteristics of one voice in this respect, of what is generally referred to in my book as *Chaucer's voice*, the voice of the presence behind the narrators and the implied authors (cf the discussion of Chatman's model, pp 25–6). In other words I suggest that Chaucer's voice is both everywhere and very consciously displayed, whether it is playful, serious, evoking pathos or despairing.

Turning to narration in *The Knight's Tale*, the discussion in chapter 2 is first of all centered on the persona-interpretations that still characterize most critical treatments of the tale. The most extreme of these is no doubt Terry Jones' from 1979, which in its time provoked some needed scholarly response. I have similar ambitions when postulating that many of the critics discussed in chapter two fall in a trap prepared by Jones by counting on Chaucer's ironical distance to the Knight-narrator. The myth about the *Canterbury Tales*-personae is indeed a hardlived one, and we need critical effort to counter it. I contend that the solution is not to shout from the opposite corner that Chaucer himself can be identified with more or less all narrators, as we have seen a few critics maintain. Nuanced analysis of the often inconsistent narrative voice, including some persona-narration, is called for instead.

In *The Knight's Tale* the Knight-persona is obviously present in the frame of the tale, and the story-matter is suited for his social position. Apart from that my analysis has shown that the narration represents various shades of the Chaucerian voice recognizable elsewhere in his works, and that particularly in the *visio* of book III it makes little sense to operate with a Knight-narrator. Likewise the discourse is far too complicated to be given a general label such as 'archaic' or 'pathriarchal' (see p 43). The narrator is not even an open persona (cf the discussion of Lawton and Chatman, p 36), because the 'character' behind the discourse cannot, however hard we try, be identified with the Knight from *The General Prologue* without distorting the image of a fighting man with supposedly no primary bookish interests. What we hear is clearly Chaucer's educated voice, in many instances giving cross-references to his own work and to a great number of his sources.

It is another matter that Chaucer deliberately lets his narrator adopt a different general stance from other of his distinct narrators, notably the one in *Troilus and Criseyde*. In chapter 3 the poetic design and narrative strategy are established on the basis of a comparison with Boccaccio's *Teseida*. Chaucer's version is indeed a poem in its own right, especially because of the structuring of material and the narration. The narrator adopts a detached position in relation to the lovers, much unlike Boccaccio's version, and the structure and pace of the poem are significantly altered, cf Muscatine's famous phrase, 'a poetic pageant'. The three approaches represented by respectively Thurston, Kolve and Brewer, the last of these in my adaption on the basis of Jakobson, explain the structuring principle in alternative ways: as either 'incongruous and episodical', as centered around images of prison/garden contrasts, or as connected by metonymic and metaphorical relations. I advocate all these as enlightening analyses of poetic and narrative design and offer my own general model for structural analysis from the angle of narrative as a supplement (see p 51). The model is built around contrasts in the narrative stance and serves as a framework for the analysis in chapters 5–7.

The main analysis of narrative voice, part II, starts with a consideration of narratorial self-consciousness and direct presence in the tale. The comparison with popular romances makes it abundantly clear that the voicing is quite distinct and unconventional, and we see further how Chaucer makes the voice a point in itself in this and earlier poems. No doubt Chaucer enjoyed exhibiting his poetic skills, as in many of the eloquent *occupatios*, but the function of narratorial self-display is more than an artist's promotion of himself. We see in the analysis how the narrative is often structured around narratorial intervention and how Chaucer imposes control of his material – and (presumably) of his audience. I claim with Derek Pearsall that the technique is taken beyond reasonable limits a few times, particularly in the long occupatio describing the funeral rites and in the rendering of Arcite's death, but the importance of these discrepancies should not be overestimated. We must not forget that Chaucer is operating on the balance of a knife's edge with his forceful visual and narrative effects, and if the intended humorous relief does not work in a few cases it is understandable. However, it remains a paradox that even crude realism, like that of Theseus, can provide relief, as pointed out by Salter (see pp 69–70). Such is also the nature of the best and most consistent narratorial joke, the general plea of ignorance concerning divination, philosophy and the pagan world.

The reason why such relief is needed is spelled out in my analysis in chapters 6 and 7. High seriousness and high rhetoric go hand in hand in the representations of the pagan deities and Boethian philosophy, and particularly the temple scene at the beginning of book III depicts a bleak and desolate vision of the pagan universe. This *visio* is rendered in the first-person form that Chaucer knew so well from his early poetic career, but the composition and visual effect are sharpened in comparison with the earlier works, and the whole passage is made to tie up with central motifs and themes in the poem: isolation, ill Fortune, emptiness, lack of mercy. The mood and tone of book III alone make it reasonable to talk about the predominance of a dark serious key in the poem.

The philosophical complaints of Palamon and Arcite at the end of book one are more than justified in the light of the later representation of the cruel gods and the ensuing tragedy, but it is a major dramatic irony that the speeches are not in fact delivered in that context. The narrator remains silent, but Chaucer's hidden voice makes it clear that the two lovers have gone astray and are quite helpless in their suffering. The inserted Boethian philosophy is put in the mouths of characters who are not in a position to understand its premises and conclusions. The Christian consolation is never made accessible for either of the lovers, but after reaching a lowest level in the fight outside the grove, breaking their oaths of sworn brother-hood, both are shown after the fatal tournament to have become ennobled by their experiences. Arcite may not die a hero's death, but he stoically accepts his lot and is able to seek reconciliation with Palamon. The pathos of Arcite's dying speech is remarkable.

The pathos is reinforced by the striking image of pilgrims passing to and fro in Egeus' speech, which turns out to be a piece of political pragmatism rather than a philosophical consolation. In my argument in chapter 7 I rely heavily on evidence gathered from a comparison with Chaucer's handling of Theseus elsewhere in his poetry, which makes it apparent that his figure is not unequivocally positive in Chaucer's mythological perception. To my knowledge my evidence has not been used before in criticism, but especially the portrayal of Theseus as it emerges in *The Legend of Good Women* makes it hard to believe that the Muscatine-tradition is right in its celebration of this ruler. Evidence in *The Knight's Tale* itself, such as Theseus' rash behaviour and sometimes vulgar language, puts a question mark to his character, although his qualities as a duke and ruler are not challenged, just as is the case in the other poems.

This is why 'the assurance is deceptive' (Salter, see p 98). The central philosophical problems in the poem are left unresolved because of the premises given for them, ie because of the lack of Christian consolation. It is thus an open rather than a closed denouement we find at the end of *The Knight's Tale*, and maybe this has a further significance, since it is the first tale. Chaucer spends many of the following tales exploring the human situation in multiple variations on themes raised in this tale: not only friendship, love and marriage, but also questions of man's place in the universe and the meaning of faith, hope and charity. In other words the big questions concerning the meaning of life – and death and the afterlife – but let me stress that I do not regard the explicitly Christian tales, eg *The Second Nun's Tale*, *Melibee* and *The Parson's Tale* as sole exponents of the answers. No doubt in Chaucer's universe the Christian doctrine has undisputed priority, but what makes Chaucer so particularly remarkable in his time is his foregrounding of the human experience. William Blake talked of 'the great poetical observer of men' and of 'a master and father, and superior, who looks down on their little follies' (see p 10). This is accurate, even though it is Troilus, not himself (or Arcite for that matter) that Chaucer has ascend to the eighth sphere to have such a vantage position.

It is here that the 'paradoxical sense of distance and closeness' comes into the picture once more. Chaucer is able to evoke intimacy with the characters of his tales, while at the same time assuming a narratorial stance a certain distance away. It has been the aim of this study to show how it is possible to achieve the most subtle poetic and narrative effects – and such true pathos – by apparently simple means. Chaucer's narrative voice is the key to an explanation.

# Bibliography

## Texts, editions, primary sources:

Bennett, J. A. W., ed., *The Knight's Tale*. London: Harrap, 1954.

Benson, Larry D., ed., *The Riverside Chaucer*. Boston: Houghton Mifflin, 1987.

Bieler. Ludovicus, ed., *Boethius, De Consolatione Philosophiae*. Turnholti: *Corpus Christiano-rum* series Latina XCIV, 1957.

Blake, N. F., ed., *The Canterbury Tales edited from the Hengwrt manuscript*.London: Edward Arnold, 1980.

Blake, William, *A Descriptive Catalogue*, London, 1809.

Branca, Vittore, ed., *Tutte le Opere di Giovanni Boccaccio*. Maggio: Arnoldo Mandadori, 1964, II.

Brewer, D. S., ed., *Chaucer: The Critical Heritage, I–II*. London: Routledge & Kegan Paul, 1978.

Crow, Martin M., and Olson, Clair C, *Chaucer Life-Records*. Oxford: Oxford University Press, 1966.

Haveley, Nick, ed., *Chaucer's Boccaccio*. Cambridge and Totowa, New Jersey: Boydell & Brewer and Rowman & Littlefield, 1980.

Kolve, V. A. and Olson, Glending, eds., *The Canterbury Tales: Nine Tales and the General Prologue*. A Norton Critical Edition, New York and London: W. W. Norton & Company, 1989.

Manly, John M. and Rickert, Edith, *The Text of The Canterbury Tales, Studied on the Basis of All Known Manuscripts*. Oxford: Oxford University Press, 1940.

McCoy, Bernadette Marie, trans., *The Book of Theseus: Teseida delle Nozze d'Emilia, by Giovanni Boccaccio*. New York: Medieval Text Association, 1974.

Mills, Maldwyn, ed., *Six Middle English Romances*. London: Dent Everyman's Library, 1973.

Moseley, Charles, ed., *Geoffrey Chaucer: The Knight's Tale*. Harmondsworth: Penguin, 1987.

Pollard, A. W., ed., *The Knight's Tale*. London: MacMillan, 1903.

Robinson, F. N., ed. *The Complete Works of Geoffrey Chaucer*, 2nd ed. Oxford: Oxford University Press, 1957.

de Selincourt, Ernest, ed., *Early Letters of William & Dorothy Wordsworth, 1787–1805*. Oxford: At the Clarendon Press, 1935.

Spearing, A. C., ed., *The Knight's Tale*. Cambridge: Cambridge University Press, 1966.

## Critical books and general background:

Alexander, Michael, *York Notes on the Knight's Tale*. Burnt Mill, Harrow, Essex: Longman York Press, 1981, 2nd ed., 1990.

Aers, David, *Chaucer*. Brighton: Harvester New Readings, 1986.

Aers, David, *Chaucer, Langland, and the Creative Imagination*. London: Routledge and Kegan Paul, 1980.

Anderson, David, *Before The Knight's Tale: Imitation of Classical Epic in Boccaccio's Teseida*. Philadelphia:University of Pennsylvania Press, 1988.

Andrew, Malcolm, ed., *Critical Essays on Chaucer's Canterbury Tales*. Milton Keynes: Open University Press, 1991.

Baldwin, Ralph, *The Unity of the Canterbury Tales. Anglistica 5*; Copenhagen: Rosenkilde & Bagger, 1955.

Baum, Paul F., *Chaucer: A Critical Appreciation*. Durham: Duke University Press, 1958.

Benson, C. David., *Chaucer's Drama of Style*. Chapel Hill: North Carolina Press,1986.

Birney, Earle, *Essays on Chaucerian Irony*. Edited with an introduction by Beryl Rowland. Toronto: University of Toronto Press, 1985.

Bishop, Ian, *The Narrative Art of the Canterbury Tales: A Critical Study of the Major Poems*. London: Dent, Everyman, 1987.

Blamires, Alcuin, *The Canterbury Tales: The Critics Debate*. Houndsmill and London: MacMillan, 1987.

Boitani, P., ed., *Chaucer and the Italian Trecento*. Cambridge: Cambridge University Press, 1983.

Boitani, P. and Mann, J., *The Cambridge Chaucer Companion*. Cambridge: Cambridge University Press, 1986.

Booth, Wayne C., *The Rhetoric of Fiction*. Chicago: University of Chicago Press, 1961.

Brewer, Derek, *Chaucer: The Poet as Storyteller*. Houndsmill and London: Macmillan, 1984.

Brewer, Derek, *Chaucer: An Introduction*. London: Longman, 1984.

Brewer, D. S., *Chaucer*. Burnt Mill, Harrow, Essex: Longman, 1953 and 1970.

Brown, Peter and Butcher, Andrew, *The Age of Saturn*. Oxford: Basil Blackwell, 1991.

Burlin, Robert B., *Chaucerian Fiction*. Princeton: Princeton University Press, 1977.

Burrow, J. A., *Medieval Writers and Their Work: Middle English Literature and its Background 1100–1500*. Oxford: Oxford University Press, 1982.

Burrow, J. A., *Ricardian Poetry*. London: Routledge and Kegan Paul, 1971.

Chatman, Seymour, *Story and Discourse: Narrative Structure in Fiction and Film*. Ithaca and London: Cornell University Press, 1978.

Cooper, Helen, *The Structure of the Canterbury Tales*. Athens: University of Georgia Press and London: Duckworth, 1983.

Cooper, Helen, *The Canterbury Tales*. Oxford: Clarendon Press, *Oxford Guides to Chaucer*, 1989.

Crane, R. S., *The Languages of Criticism and the Structures of Poetry*. Toronto: University of Toronto Press, 1953.

Cummings, Hubert M., *The Indebtedness of Chaucer's Works to the Italian Works of Boccaccio*. New York: Haskell House, 1965.

Curry, Walter Clyde, *Chaucer and the Medieval Sciences*. London: Oxford University Press, 2nd revised edition, New York: Barnes & Noble, 1960.

David, Alfred, *The Strumpet Muse*. Bloomington: Indiana University Press, 1976.

Dillon, Janette, *Geoffrey Chaucer*. Houndsmill and London: MacMillan, *Writers in Their Time*, 1993.

Dinshaw, Carolyn, *Chaucer's Sexual Poetics*. Madison: University of Wisconsin Press, 1989.

Donaldson, E. Talbot, *Speaking of Chaucer*. London: The Athlone Press, University of London, 1970.

Dor, Juliette, ed., *A Wyf Ther Was: Essays in Honour of Paule Mertens-Fonck*. Liege: University of Liege, 1992.

Elbow, Peter, *Oppositions in Chaucer*. Middletown: Wesleyan University Press, 1973.

Erzgräber, Willi, ed., *Geoffrey Chaucer*. Darmstadt: Wissenschaftliche Buchgesellschaft, 1983.

Fichte, ed., *Chaucer's Frame Tales*. Tübingen: Günter Narr Verlag & Cambridge: D. S. Brewer, 1985.

Given-Wilson, Chris, *Chronicles of the Revolution 1397–1400: The Reign of Richard II*. Manchester: Manchester University Press, 1993.

Howard, Donald R., *Chaucer: His Life, His Works, His World*. New York: Dutton, 1987.

Howard, Donald R., *The Idea of the Canterbury Tales*. Berkeley: University of California Press, 1976.

Jefferson, Bernard L., *Chaucer and the Consolation of Philosophy of Boethius*. Princeton: Princeton University Press, 1973.

Jones, Terry, *Chaucer's Knight*. London: Eyre Methuen, 1980.

Jordan, Robert M., *Chaucer and the Shape of Creation*. Cambridge: Cambridge University Press, 1967.

Kean, Patricia, *The Art of Narrative: Chaucer and the Making of English Poetry*, I & II. London: Routledge and Kegan Paul, 1972.

Keen, Maurice, *Chivalry*. New Haven, Conn.: Yale University Press, 1984.

Keen, Maurice, *England in the Later Middle Ages*. London: Routledge, 1973.

Kendrick, Laura, *Chaucerian Play: Comedy and Control in the Canterbury Tales*. Berkeley: University of California Press, 1988.

Kinney, Clare Regan, *Strategies of Poetic Narrative: Chaucer, Spenser, Milton, Eliot*. Cambridge: Cambridge University Press, 1992.

Klitgård, Ebbe, *Chaucer's Knight's Tale: An Analysis with Special Reference to Theme and Philosophy*. Unpublished MA thesis, University of York, 1984.

Knapp, Peggy, *Chaucer and the Social Contest*. New York and London: Routledge, 1990.

Knight, Stephen, *Geoffrey Chaucer*. Oxford: Blackwell, 1986.

Koff, Leonard M., *Chaucer and the Art of Storytelling*. Berkeley & L. A.: University of California Press, 1988.

Kolve, V. A., *Chaucer and the Imagery of Narrative*, London: Edward Arnold, 1984.

Lawton, David, *Chaucer's Narrators*. Cambridge: D. S. Brewer, 1985.

Lewis, C. S., *The Allegory of Love: A Study in Medieval Tradition*. Oxford: Oxford University Press, 1936, repr. 1958 and 1979.

Lodge, David, *The Modes of Modern Writing*. London: Edward Arnold, 1977.

Lumiansky, R. M., *Of Sondry Folk: The Dramatic Principle in the Canterbury Tales*. Austin: University of Texas Press, 1955, repr. 1980.

MacFarlane, K. B., *Lancastrian Kings and Lollard Knights*. Oxford: Clarendon Press, 1972.

Mandel, Jerome, *Geoffrey Chaucer: Building the Fragments of the Canterbury Tales*.London and Toronto: Associated University Press, 1993.

Mann, Jill, *Chaucer and Medieval Estates Satire: The Literature of Social Classes and the General Prologue to the Canterbury Tales*. Cambridge: Cambridge University Press, 1973.

Mann, Jill, *Geoffrey Chaucer*. Hemel Hampstead: Harvester Wheatsheaf, *Feminist Readings*, 1991.

Minnis, Alistair, *Medieval Theory of Authorship: Scholastic Literary Attitudes in the Later Middle Ages*. London: Scholar Press, 1984.

Minnis, A. J. and Scott, A. B., eds., *Medieval Literary Theory and Criticism c. 1100–c. 1375: The Commentary Tradition*. Oxford and New York: Clarendon Press and Oxford University Press, 1988.

Mogan, Joseph J., *Chaucer and the Theme of Mutability*.The Hague and Paris: Mouton, 1969.

Morse, R. & Windeatt, B., eds., *Chaucer Traditions: Studies in Honour of Derek Brewer*. Cambridge: Cambridge University Press, 1990.

Muscatine, Charles, *Chaucer and the French Tradition: A Study in Style and Meaning*. Berkeley and L. A.: University of California Press, 1957.

Neuse, Richard, *Chaucer's Dante: Allegory and Epic Theater in The Canterbury Tales*. Berkeley and L. A.: University of California Press, 1991.

Nolan, Barbara, *Chaucer and the Tradition of the Roman Antique*. Cambridge: *Cambridge Studies in Medieval Literature*, 15, 1992.

Olson, Paul A., *The Canterbury Tales and the Good Society*. Princeton: Princeton University Press, 1986.

Payne, F. Anne, *Chaucer and Menippean Satire*. Madison: University of Wisconsin Press, 1981.

Patterson, Lee, *Chaucer and the Subject of History*. London: Routledge, 1991.

Pearsall, Derek, *The Canterbury Tales*. London: Allen & Unwin, 1985.

Pearsall, Derek, *The Life of Geoffrey Chaucer*. Oxford: Blackwell, 1992.

Robertson, D. W., *A Preface to Chaucer*. Princeton: Princeton University Press, 1962.

Robinson, Ian, *Chaucer and the English Tradition*. Cambridge: Cambridge University Press, 1972.

Root, Robert Kilburn, *The Poetry of Chaucer*. Boston: Houghton, Mifflin, 1922.

Roney, Lois, *Chaucer's Knight's Tale and Theories of Scholastic Psychology*. Tampa: University of South Florida Press, 1990.

Rose, D., ed., *New Perspectives in Chaucer Criticism*. Oklahoma: Pilgrim Books, 1981.

Ruggiers, Paul G., *The Art of the Canterbury Tales*. Madison and London: University of Wisconsin Press, 1967.

Salter, Elisabeth, *Chaucer: The Knight's Tale and the Clerk's Tale*. London: Edward Arnold, 1962.

Salter, Elisabeth, *Fourteenth-Century English Poetry: Contexts and Readings*. Oxford: Clarendon Press, 1983.

Schoeck, Richard J. and Taylor, Jerome, eds., *Chaucer Criticism,* 2 vols. Notre Dame and London: University of Notre Dame Press, 1960–61.

Somerville, Angus A., *Chaucer's Treatment of the Narrator and a Comparative Study of other Medieval Texts*. Unpublished Ph. D.-thesis, Glasgow University, 1969.

Spearing, A. C., *Medieval to Renaissance in English Poetry*. Cambridge: Cambridge University Press, 1985.

Strohm, Paul, *Social Chaucer*. Cambridge: Harvard University Press, 1989.

Thurston, Paul T., *Artistic Ambivalence in Chaucer's Knight's Tale*. Gainesville: University of Florida Press, 1968.

Twycross, Meg, *The Medieval Anadyomene*. Oxford: *Medium Ævum monographs*, 1972.

Wagenknecht, Edward, ed., *Chaucer: Modern Essays in Criticism*. New York: Oxford University Press, 1959.

Weinberg, Julius R., *A Short History of Medieval Philosophy*. Princeton: Princeton University Press, 1964.

Whittock, Trevor, *A Reading of the Canterbury Tales*. Cambridge: Cambridge University Press, 1968.

Wimsatt, James, *Chaucer and His French Contemporaries*. Toronto: Toronto Press, 1991.

Yeager, R. F., ed., *Chaucer and Gower: Difference, Mutuality, Exchange*. Victoria: University of Victoria, *English Literary Studies*, 1991.

## Articles:

Aers, David, 'Criseyde: Woman in Medieval Society.' *The Chaucer Review*, 13, 1979.

Aers, David, review of Terry Jones, *Chaucer's Knight*. *Studies in the Age of Chaucer*, 4, 1982.

Blake, Katleen A., 'Order and the Noble Life in Chaucer's *Knight's Tale*?' *Modern Language Quarterly,* 34, 1973.

Bloomfield, Morton W., 'Authenticating Realism and the Realism of Chaucer.' *Thought*, 34, 1964. Also reprinted in Erzgräber, *op. cit.*

Bloomfield, Morton W., 'Contemporary Literary Theory and Chaucer.' Repr. in Rose, *op. cit.*

Boitani, Piero, 'Style, Iconography and Narrative: the Lesson of the *Teseida.*' Repr. in Boitani, ed., *op. cit.*

Brooks, D., and Fowler, A., 'The Meaning of Chaucer's *Knight's Tale.*' *Medium Ævum*, 1970.

Burrow, J., 'Chaucer and the Three Ages of Man.' Burrow, ed., *Essays on Medieval Literature.* Oxford: Clarendon Press, 1984.

Børch, Marianne, 'Poet & Persona; Writing the reader in *Troilus.*' Sauerberg, ed., *Papers Presented to Andreas Haarder.* Odense: *Pre-Publications of the English Department of Odense University*, 1994.

Cooper, Helen, 'The Shape-shiftings of the Wife of Bath, 1395–1670.' Repr. in Morse & Windeatt, eds., *op. cit.*

Cowgill, Bruce C., '*The Knight's Tale* and the 100 Years War.' *Philological Quarterly*, 54, 1975.

Crane, Susan, 'Medieval Romance and Feminine Difference in *The Knight's Tale.*' *Studies in the Age of Chaucer*, 12, 1990.

Dent, A. A., 'Chaucer and the Horse.' *Proceedings of the Leeds Philosophical and Literary Society*, IX, 1952–62.

Finlayson, John, '*The Knight's Tale*: The Dialogue of Romance, Epic, and Philosophy.' *The Chaucer Review*, 27, 1992.

Frost, 'An Interpretation of Chaucer's *Knight's Tale.*' *Review of English Studies*, 25, 1949.

Heltermann, Jeffrey, 'The Dehumanizing Metamorphoses of the *Knight's Tale.*' *English Literary History*, 38, 1971.

Herzman, 'The Paradox of Form: *The Knight's Tale* and Chaucerian Aesthetics.' *Papers on Language and Literature*, 10, 1974. Also reprinted in Erzgräber, *op. cit.*

Jakobson, Roman, 'Two Aspects of Language and Two Types of Aphasic Disturbances.' Repr. in Jakobson,*Selected Writings*, vol. II. The Hague and Paris: Mouton, 1971.

Jakobson, Roman, 'Closing Statement: Linguistics and Poetics.' Repr. in Sebeok, Thomas A., ed., *Style in Language.* New York and London: Technology Press of Massachusetts Institute of Technology and John Wiley & Sons, 1960.

Knapp, Peggy A., 'Deconstructing *The Canterbury Tales*: pro.' *Studies in the Age of Chaucer*, 9, 1987. Repr. in Andrew, *op. cit.*

Keen, Maurice, 'Chaucer's Knight, the English Aristocracy and the Crusade.' Scattergood and Sherbourne, eds., *English Court Culture in the Later Middle Ages.* London: Duckworth, 1983.

Kittredge, G. L., 'Chaucer's Discussion of Marriage.' *Modern Philology*, 9, 1912. Also repr. in Andrew, *op. cit.*

Klitgård, Ebbe, 'Chaucer and Modern Criticism'. *Engelsk Meddelelser,*1993.

Lawler, Traugott, 'Deconstructing *The Canterbury Tales*: con.' *Studies in the Age of Chaucer*, 9, 1987. Repr. in Andrew, *op. cit.*

Leicester Jr., H. Marshall, 'The Art of Impersonation: A General Prologue to the *Canterbury Tales.*' *Publications of the Modern Language Association of America*, 95, 1980. Also repr. in Andrew and in Kolve and Olson, *op. cit.*

Lester, G. A., 'Chaucer's Knight and the Medieval Tournament.' *Neophilogus*, 66, 1982.

Lewis, C. S., 'What Chaucer really did to *Il Filostrato.*' *Essays and Studies by Members of the English Association*, xvii, 1932.

Lodge, David, 'The Language of Modernist Fiction: Metaphor and Metonymy.' Bradbury and McFarlane, eds., *Modernism 1890–1930.* Hammondsworth: Penguin, 1976.

Lumiansky, R. M., 'Chaucer's Philosophical Knight.' *Tulane Studies in English*, III, 1952.

Luxon, Thomas H., '"Sentence" and "Solas": Proverbs and Consolation in the *Knight's Tale*.' *The Chaucer Review*, 22, 1987.

Manly, John Matthews, 'A Knight Ther Was.' *Transactions and Proceedings of the American Philological Association*, 1907. Also repr. in Wagenknecht, *op. cit.*

Mann, Jill, 'Chance and Destiny in *Troilus and Criseyde* and the *Knight's Tale*. Repr. in Boitani and Mann, *op. cit.*

Marckwardt, A. H., 'Characterization in Chaucer's *Knight's Tale*.' *University of Michigan Contributions in Modern Philology*, 5, 1947.

Martin, Priscilla, 'Chaucer and Feminism: A Magpie View.' Dor, ed., *A Wyf Ther Was: Essays in Honour of Paule Mertens-Fonck*. Liege: University of Liege, 1992.

Mehl, Dieter, 'Erscheinungsformen des Erzählers in Chaucers *Canterbury Tales*.' Arno Esch, ed., *Chaucer und seine Zeit. Symposium für Walter Schirmer*. Tübingen: Niemeyer, 1968. Repr. in Erzgräber, *op. cit.*

Minnis, Alistair, 'Chaucer and Comtemporary Literary Theory.' Repr. in Rose, *op. cit.*

Mitchell, Charles, 'The Worthiness of Chaucer's Knight.' *Modern Language Quarterly*, 25, 1964.

Muscatine, Charles, 'Form, Texture and Meaning in Chaucer's *Knight's Tale.*' Wagenknecht, *op. cit.* Originally printed in *Publications of the Modern Language Association of America*, LXV, 1950.

Neuse, Richard, 'The Knight: The First Mover in Chaucer's Human Comedy.' *University of Toronto Quarterly*, 31, 1962.

Nolan, Barbara, '"A Poet Ther Was": Chaucer's Voices in the General Prologue to *The Canterbury Tales*.' *Publications of the Modern Language Association of America*, 101, 1986.

Oliver, Paul, 'Ambiguous Icons: Chaucer's Knight, Parson and Plowman.' Cockson and Loughrey, eds., *Critical Essays on the General Prologue to the Canterbury Tales*, (London: Longman, 1989).

Olsson, Kurt, 'Securitas and Chaucer's Knight.' *Studies in the Age of Chaucer*, 9, 1987.

Pearsall, Derek, 'Chaucer's Poetry and its Modern Commentators: The Necessity of History.' Aers, David, ed., *Medieval Literature*. Brighton: Harvester Press, 1986.

Pratt, John H., 'Was Chaucer's Knight Really a Mercenary?' *The Chaucer Review*, 22, 1, 1987.

Ridley, Florence, 'A Response to "Contemporary Literary Theory and Chaucer."' Repr. in Rose, *op. cit.*

Robertson, Jr., D. W., 'The Probable Date and Purpose of Chaucer's *Knight's Tale*.' *Studies in Philology*, 84, 1987.

Robertson, Stuart, 'Elements of Realism in the *Knight's Tale*.' *Journal of English and Germanic Philology*, 14, 1915.

Schweitzer, Edward C., 'Fate and Freedom in the Knight's Tale.' *Studies in the Age of Chaucer*, 3, 1981.

Smith, James, 'Chaucer, Boethius, and Recent Trends in Criticism.' *Essays in Criticism*, 22, 1972.

Strauss, Jennifer, '"I kan nat seye": The Rhetoric of Narratorial Self- consciousness in Chaucer, Especially in *The Canterbury Tales*.' *AUMLA. Journal of the Australasian Language and Literature Association*, May 1988.

Underwood, Dale, 'The First of the *Canterbury Tales*.' *English Literary History*, 36, 1959.

Wetherbee, Winthrop, 'Convention and Authority: A Comment on Some Recent Critical Approaches to Chaucer.' Repr. in Rose, *op. cit.*

Yeager, R. F., 'Pax Poetica: On the Pacifism of Chaucer & Gower.' *Studies in the Age of Chaucer*, 1987.

D

DIS